Happy Sales to you!

A. Bleer

The New Language of Sales

A radically different conversation

By Willa Silver

The New Language of Sales
By Willa Silver

Copyright Notices:

Coaching to the Human Soul, Ontological Coaching, and Deep Change Volumes I and II, by Alan Sieler

Language and the Pursuit of Happiness, by Chalmers Brothers

The Psychology of Sales Call Reluctance: Earning What You're Worth in Sales by George W. Dudley and Shannon L. Goodson, ©2007, Behavioral Sciences Research Press, Inc., Dallas, Texas. USED WITH PERMISSION.

Book design by David Wineberg
Cover graphic by Deborah Benoit

Silver, Willa
The new Language of Sales A Radically Different Conversation, by Willa Silver
1. Sales Training
2. Self improvement
3. Ontology
ISBN: 978-0-9878844-0-4

In this book I will show you at every point in the process, how an Ontological approach to sales not only differs from what they hammered into your head all your life, but also how you can take those differences and employ them to your sales advantage.
And your clients will love you for it!

Table of Contents

The New Language of Sales

A radically different conversation

Acknowledgement

For much of my adult life I was the poster child for Oppositional Reflex: a hard-edged type of sales call reluctance characterized by the need for continuous feedback which is then criticized and rejected as invalid. Such salespeople are unable to allow themselves to be coached, advised, managed or trained. I was successful in spite of myself.

My sincere apologies to all the coaches and trainers to whom I gave such a hard time.

My life expanded exponentially when I found the profession of coaching and the discipline of Ontology.

My thanks and gratitude to all the pioneers in this realm of thought. The list is large but includes: Fernando Flores, Humberto Maturana, Werner Erhard, Francisco Varela, Julio Olalla, and my deepest thanks to Alan Sieler and Chalmers Brothers for their generosity in allowing me to quote so many passages from their books that it became impossible to note each quote in footnotes.

My thanks to all the accredited coach training organizations such as The Coaches Training Institute and Newfield Coach Training for their commitment to education and to the International Coach Federation for their dedication to advancing the coaching profession.

Thanks to Wolfgang for giving me the gift of knowing I'm not the only Ontological Sales Coach on the planet. Let's stand in the possibility that there will be many more of us to follow.

I wish I could claim ownership of many of the insights I'll be describing in this book, but alas, I have a 30 year background in sales and was and still am putting all my energy into sales coaching. The credit belongs to my predecessors.

My commitment is to share these powerful and effective insights with my world, the world of sales, with the absolute knowledge that they will make a difference to every sales conversation we have, giving us all access to greater success.

Introduction

I have always wondered why the profession of Sales has such a negative perception and why I could never really embrace traditional sales training. In fact, traditional sales training had the opposite effect; it put me off. Through my coach training I can see how the old model of the sales "process" is manipulative and agenda driven. Most people are savvy to sales "strategies" and sick and tired of being at the receiving end of those kinds of conversations. Most sales professionals are also sick and tired of those conversations and would agree they do not produce the level of results they really want.

A good friend of mine who is a real estate agent expressed her frustration with this really well. She felt that there had to be a better way than following the herd that uses the old mind frame of sales. She feels it has done a disservice to the world and that all sales people are viewed the same way – "All you want to do is sell me something." She actually referred to the way real estate agents are viewed as a "swarm of locusts!"

I am committed to transforming the negative perception of sales to the noble profession I truly believe it is.

This is a very big undertaking and a bold commitment.

How do you eat an elephant? One bite at a time.

How do you transform the perception of sales? One conversation at a time.

Sales is a series of conversations, nothing more, nothing less. Once we begin to understand all the elements that are present in an engaging and enrolling conversation, sales becomes so much simpler.

Have you noticed the *effort* it takes to think of the right question to uncover the pain, the *effort* it takes to make your value proposition understood, the *effort* it takes to communicate features and benefits, the *effort* it takes to handle objections, the *effort* it takes to close for the business? Let all that go.

By learning about and practicing *active listening techniques*, intentional questions will present themselves. Meaningful offers and effective requests will lead to commitment and action from your prospects producing breakthrough results.

You will find that the same concepts/distinctions showing up in different parts of the book. If it sounds like I'm repeating myself, I am. Think of it as: how does this concept apply in this particular point of the sales conversation? It's through mastery of all these interlocking concepts that you will make yourself a true Sales Professional.

This is how you will differentiate yourself from any other sales rep or telemarketer your prospects have had to suffer through.

1

Being, or What the &^$%#* is Ontology?

J ust taking action to do things differently seldom works. Knowing why, how and what to change can increase your chances of success, but to sustain any change you have to "be" different, not "know" or "do" different things. We all have good intentions, but they tend to "break down" after a while because we are still "being" the same, doing the same things, which leads to having the same results. This is not about changing your identity or personality; it's about a new way of seeing yourself and the world you operate in. To change your way of being you start by observing your language, mood and body state. An Ontological Coach knows how to guide you in challenging the long-held assumptions and beliefs about life and work that are holding you back from being all you can be.

So what the @$%&# is Ontology?

I'll keep this short, sweet and respectful that you didn't buy a book on philosophy.

Ontology is the study of Being and the inquiry into the nature of human existence. This inquiry revolves around a central question: "What does it mean to be a human being?" The question that my readers might have is "What the heck does that mean to me as a sales professional, and why should I care?"

Well, I'm assuming that you and your prospects are fully human and by having insights as to how you are both hardwired will give you greater access to effective interactions and increase your odds of reaching your full potential.

Ontology focuses on our *Way of Being*. This expression should not be equated with behaviour. Way of Being refers to how we observe or perceive the world. How we observe things (e.g. events, circumstances, people and objects) reflects our Way of Being.

This means that observing is not merely a passive activity. Our Way of Being, or how we observe things, drives our behaviours, which produces our results in life.

The interaction of our Way of Being and observing shapes our behaviour. We act and react on how we observe circumstances. Our Way of Being can be largely invisible to us, operating beneath the surface of our daily existence, yet having the power to run our lives and shape how we perceive and respond to situations. Our Way of Being silently and invisibly informs us how to observe and engage with the world.

Much of our dissatisfaction in life stems from not being able to act or behave in ways that produce the results we want.

The principles of Ontology expand our Way of Being so that more possibilities become available, thus opening up new experiences and an enrichment of the process of living and being human.

These principles live in three realms: language, emotion and body. Sales lives in these three realms as well. Sales is simply a series of conversations and conversations consist of the words we choose: our language. If we look at the words we typically use in sales, we can see that they are based on getting, convincing or influencing people to do something we want them to do. With that approach, who we are Being is self-serving and manipulative. I believe this is the root of the negative perception of sales professionals. Once we shift our language and Way of Being we will begin to shift the perception of sales and begin to shift how we interact with our prospects.

We all know people buy on emotion, yet most of us are reluctant to fully dive into this realm. It is typically an area of discomfort. You may ask a few questions to identify what's important to your prospect, but stop when you "think" you have found it. That isn't where you jot down a quick note and go on to the next topic of conversation; that's actually the beginning of a meaningful conversation. Noticing their emotions and being willing to explore that will dramatically increase your odds of bringing on a new client.

At a recent workshop, a participant asked if there was a good book they could read about the psychology of their prospect. My answer was simple: it doesn't start with knowing more about your prospect's emotional responses; it starts by understanding your own. It doesn't live externally; it all starts between your own ears. If you are uncomfortable in a particular area, you will never fully explore that with your prospect, potentially limiting the effectiveness of your offers and requests. If you are willing to practice in this realm, you will have an advantage over most of your competition.

As a culture, we are not taught to embrace emotions. On the contrary, we are taught to suppress them, causing no end of problems. At no time in history have more people experienced such levels of dissatisfaction in life and suffered from this much depression. The sheer volume of people taking antidepressants is a testimonial to that sad state of affairs.

We are also taught the importance of reading body language. What they've never taught is what goes on behind the surface that drives each conversation. After all, there are two human beings interacting with one another in sales, and if I can give you deeper levels of understanding as to what is happening for you and your prospect, you will be able to take your sales conversations to the next level of effectiveness.

Many principles from Ontology have trickled into our everyday lives as well as into sales. You'll find that some of the things I talk about in this book sound familiar. However, what has filtered down is typically only the top layer, the veneer.

The problem with veneer is that it's weak and provides little or no surface to properly grip to. It splinters easily. This book will give you far deeper insights. We will be getting to the meat of the wood. That is where the power of these principles truly lives.

This sounds quite philosophical and for those of us who live in the world of pragmatism, it can sound a little *woo-woo*. But before we get down to brass tacks and describe how well this can increase your sales, I'd like you to examine how open you are to new approaches.

2

<u>OBSTACLES TO LEARNING</u>

No matter how much you may agree, or in particular disagree with some of the information I give you, it will be very difficult for you to incorporate a new learning into your day-to-day business if you have a barrier to learning that is hidden from your view.

Let's put a spotlight on any barriers you might have, so you will be able to choose powerfully whether or not you would like to try on some new approaches.

BARRIERS TO LEARNING

Let's do a quick check-in to see where you might have barriers in your way (if any).

Check off the boxes that align with what you notice you agree with:

☐ Declaring "I already know"

☐ Attachment to previous learning – "This is just like the training/approach I've already been taught and I like that one better"

☐ Declaring inability to learn – "I can't/couldn't do that"

☐ Living in others' assessments – "What will they think of me?"

☐ Unwilling to declare our ignorance and admit that we do not know

☐ Not allowing our self to learn from others

☐ Knowing how we *should* be taught and the way things *should* be done

☐ Heaviness and "seriosity" – making things too much of a "big deal" and being overly serious and solemn

☐ Arrogance – "I don't need to know this; nothing new for me to learn here; this is stupid; this is ridiculously simple; how could they know more than me – I'm better than them" (all disguising fear/anxiety)

☐ Anxiety – "Something bad or embarrassing could happen; better not risk it"

FRIENDS OF LEARNING

Now let's explore the attitudes that will enhance your capacity for learning.

- Declaring ignorance – "I don't know"
- Declaration of being a learner – "I don't know and I want to learn"
- Declaring a teacher – "I can and want to learn from this person"
- Declaration of legitimacy as a learner – "I'm not perfect and I am a learner"
- Making requests – "Could you please help me learn this?"
- Humility
- Curiosity and wonder
- Acceptance, patience, and practice
- Staying with being uncomfortable and unsettled about new experiences
- Determination and persistence
- Lightness and an ability to laugh at self
- Being passionate, but not obsessive, about new information

- A mood of inquiry

- Alan Sieler, *Coaching to the Human Soul, Volume I*

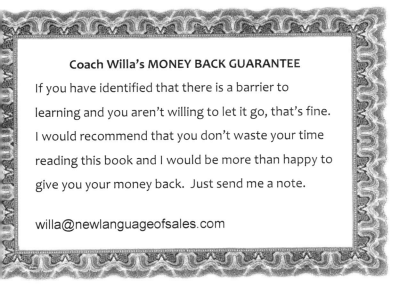

Coach Willa's MONEY BACK GUARANTEE

If you have identified that there is a barrier to learning and you aren't willing to let it go, that's fine. I would recommend that you don't waste your time reading this book and I would be more than happy to give you your money back. Just send me a note.

willa@newlanguageofsales.com

If you are open to learning, let's get the ball rolling...

3

FIRST AND SECOND ORDERS OF LEARNING

FIRST ORDER OF LEARNING

There is a common belief that your results are strongly connected to your actions. The First Order of Learning has to do with changing your actions. What come to mind for me are two very old sayings: If you always do what you've always done, you will always have what you've already got. And: the definition of insanity is doing the same thing over and over again hoping to produce different results. Much as you try to tweak, massage or increase your actions to produce breakthrough results, when you are stuck in the loop of "I'll change my actions to produce better results," your results will be limited.

This model implies that there is a problem "out there" and in order to solve it you must take actions which are effective in producing some desired result.

Our results have a great deal to do with our actions or lack of actions. This is well-known. What's less clear is that our actions themselves have a great deal to so with the observer that we are, with how we "see things".

What we don't often notice is that the way we observe, interpret, listen – the way we "see things" – comes *before* we take any action.

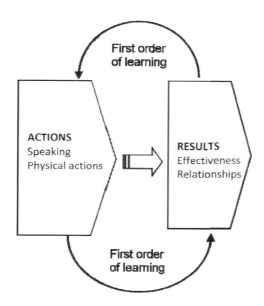

We are each unique observers, unique listeners, unique interpreters of situations. We bring unique sets of concerns and stories to the table... and so what we see, what we observe reveals more about us than about what's "out there". What's important to notice is that you don't notice this!

The range of what we think and do is limited by what we fail to notice. And because we fail to notice that we fail to notice, there is little we can do to change until we notice how failing to notice shapes our thoughts and deeds."
-R.D. Laing

SECOND ORDER OF LEARNING

This is the essence of an Ontological approach to sales and to learning.

By noticing your own private conversations, you put yourself in the position of choice. When your private conversations are hidden from your view and/or become a belief, they own you. By noticing them, you now own them and have a choice. You can allow them to hold you back from achieving all you can, or you can notice them and act with courage by stepping out of your comfort zone and trying on new approaches. Of course, the whole notion of choice makes no difference at all if we think the way we see things = the way things truly are! The whole idea of taking a look at how we look at things is of very little value if you're convinced that you see things "objectively" and "realistically" already.

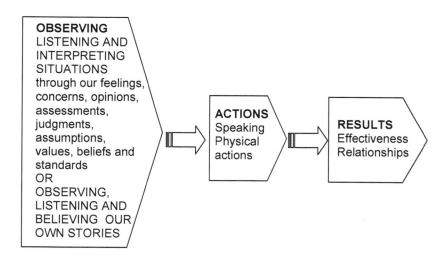

Consider the two following questions:

1. How do you actually achieve the results you achieve?
2. What actions are available to you, given that sometimes you produce results that you'd rather not produce?

There is a simple and powerful way of understanding ourselves, our actions, and our results.

This model, called the Observer-Action-Results model, was initially developed by Chris Argyris and Robert Putnam.

This model is all about how we do what we do, and get what we get.

HOW COURAGEOUS ARE YOU?

It takes more courage to take a look at how we look at things than it does to simply try new actions. Most of us would rather just pay our $299 to buy another CD to get another tip or trick that will potentially give us access to greater success in sales. Valid as this may occur, it will produce limited results. Our actions are all coming from the same perspective and beliefs, the same observations.

But if you finally look at how you look at things, you will see that you indeed have a particular "point of view". Not like it is *the* way of looking at things, but *a* way. From an Ontological point of view (not like the truth, but like a possible way of looking at things), moving forward here requires courage for most of us, because it may involve fear. Fear of change is a fundamental fear for human beings. It's uncomfortable and may require the courage to deal with the fact that our point of view may not be *the* truth, which can be confronting.

Believe it or not, many of my clients have a belief that the profession of sales is slimy, sleazy, depressing, or even beneath them.

A common example is Adam. On our second call I heard a concern behind his words and asked a lot of questions. At one point he told me when he hears the word "sales" he thinks of Death of a Salesman, Willy Loman. He gets depressed, and thinks that all sales professionals will do anything to "rope you in". Once clients identify this type of belief, one possible way of being is to resist looking at it at all. I have noticed they may forget about our coach call or schedule a meeting with a prospect for the same time. In Adam's case, he sent my assistant an email ending our coaching. He didn't have the courage to talk to me about it. We have subsequently talked through this obstacle.

When you identify a barrier, coaching can become uncomfortable. Many people would rather have someone give them another new "script" rather than address the core issue: the reason being that no matter what they seem to try to do, they do not experience long-term breakthrough results.

It takes courage to look, address and take responsibility for the common denominator in all the approaches you have tried...you.

4

THE STORIES WE TELL OURSELVES

Part of being human is to want to make sense of what we observe. We make sense of things by describing and providing explanations for our observations. We do this by developing a story and the story provides a description and explanatory framework that provides meaning. This in turn allows us to begin to develop familiarity with what was previously unfamiliar. When we make sense of something unfamiliar, we become more settled and less disoriented. Familiarity allows the world to become a more certain place for us, meeting a fundamental requirements of what it is to be human.

In his book "Language and the Pursuit of Happiness," Chalmers Brothers explains how our stories can limit our results. One of his favourite stories is about a lion:

"Let's pretend I'm a lion on the savannah, getting ready to hunt for a zebra. Behind me on my left are other young males, wishing it was their turn in the spotlight, their turn to hunt. Behind me on my right are the females, checking me out. I see the zebra I want. It's a slow one in the back. I've got mine picked out. I take a running start, get ready for the final pounce, and kaboom, I hit a hidden log and down I tumble, in a cloud of dust. Getting up, I'm thinking "I *knew* I shouldn't have had that antelope last night. It was so filling, and I knew I was scheduled to hunt today... look at them all laughing at me... I'll never be king, not with this on my record... and look at her, I can forget about our date for Saturday night... this is about the worst day in my life... I'm humiliated... in fact, I may have to join another pride!"

Key question: as far as we know, does a lion do that? I say no, a lion doesn't do that. What does a lion do? Usually the lion will get up and chase after another zebra or whatever. But *we* do that – human beings do that.

An event happens, and as human beings, very quickly:

1. We observe the event
2. We make up a story
3. We believe our story like it's *The Truth*
4. We forget that we made it up.
5. We take action in alignment with our stories

A good example of this is:

Event: I did not get the promotion I was hoping for:

Story #1: The boss is playing favourites. I was the most qualified and he simply likes Barbara better.

Action: I guess I need to start looking for another job, one where they appreciate me.

Story #2: I knew I wouldn't get it. I was probably just wasting my time even applying.

Action: I'm just not cut out to move up the ladder, I'll just stay where I am.

Story #3: Maybe there are some aspects of my performance that are perceived as negative that I'm not aware of.

Action: I'll ask my boss if he would share that with me and give me some coaching.

Story #4: Barbara probably sabotaged me by talking about me with that new client. I know that client is a golfing buddy of my boss. She's probably stirred things up.

Action: Resentment towards Barbara and a belief that as long as she's around, the likelihood of promotions are slim.

Story #5: As far as I know, Barbara has had nothing but superior client interactions. Maybe there is something I can learn from her.

Action: Schedule some time to sit down with her and ask her to share best practices.

In essence, human beings are meaning-making machines. It's part of our hardwiring. We automatically interpret any situation we experience and assign a meaning to it. We then align our actions to the meaning we made up or the story we told ourselves.

In our sales career, one of the stories we can tell ourselves is that "If they don't sign in X time, they will never sign." This story will stop you from following up and sabotage potential future sales.

The most common story I hear is "I don't have time". When I conduct workshops, I always identify the top performer and ask permission to use his/her case as an example. During this exercise I have the group create a list of obstacles to growing their business. Time management invariably comes up. I then ask the top performer if he/she has a magic watch with more than 24 hours a day on it. NO. Does he/she feel they have some superhuman power that allows them to transcend the barrier of time? NO. So, I ask the participants who identified time management as an issue, what's the difference between Mr/Ms top performer and YOU? Their story about time! A convenient excuse they made up to justify not doing the things that they feel are uncomfortable.

You can choose to be uncomfortable connecting with people, or you can choose to believe a more empowering conversation. You DO have a choice, although in the thick of things, it doesn't occur to you that you do.

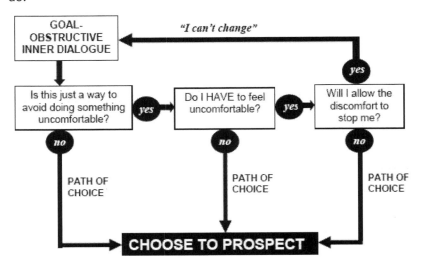

It shows up when we actually believe an objection we invented, and it stops the conversation cold.

It shows up when we tell ourselves that "I can't approach my friends. It will jeopardize our relationship."

It shows up everywhere in our sales conversations.

The moment we begin thinking that our explanation of what just happened *is* what happened, we stop listening.

5

BELIEFS CAN KILL

How your beliefs shape your sales conversations

Have you ever wondered why one sales professional does something and produces outstanding results and when another does the exact same thing produces very different results? What we have identified is that your actions and results stem from your beliefs, what you tell yourself, your private conversations. Your attitude and beliefs play a far bigger role in your success than you would ever imagine.

One example of this is a past client of mine. Cathy is a well established entrepreneur and approached me to help her get comfortable cold calling. In our first meeting I discovered she was very well connected. She was active on many boards of directors and for years had been participating in an association geared towards executives. When I asked how she capitalized on these longstanding relationships, she promptly told me she would never talk to any of them about business because she was concerned about occurring as pushy or aggressive.

BELIEF=I could occur as pushy

EVIDENCE=The people who everyone wants to avoid at networking events. The ones that practically pounce on you trying to sell you something

ACTION=None

RESULTS=None

I also have many clients who believe that the best place to start prospecting is with the people who know and trust them and are more than willing to support them in growing their business.

BELIEF=My friends and family are a great support network

ACTION=Making effective requests

RESULTS=Outstanding

Without addressing the actual obstacle to Cathy's success, a belief, I could have given her lots of homework with regards to talking to her warm market and there always would have been a good reason that she couldn't.

I worked with a company that sells high end technical software solutions. Their product and service is quite expensive, sometimes exceeding $1M. The rep who co-founded the company was uncomfortable with the high price tags and was consistently hammered on price, to the point that, with my advice, they decided to increase any of his proposals by 10-15% so he had negotiation room. The other rep had no such belief. She knew that the prices were reasonable and no one in the company was driving a Mercedes or living in a mansion. The company made a reasonable profit margin ensuring its ongoing viability and success. When she presented a proposal over the million dollar mark to a major bank, the decision maker asked if she could sharpen her pencil. She said with confidence, No. He picked up the pen and signed. The only difference between the two reps was their belief.

Many times our beliefs are hidden from our own view. This is simply how human beings are designed. Until we can actually see the obstacle to success we are destined to get to a certain point in our success and then hit a wall.

Here's another example of two sales professionals performing the exact same actions yet producing very different results.

Why is it that two sales professionals can sit on the phone and make hundreds of dials each week, one scheduling meeting after meeting and the other producing little or no results?

Could it be the list they are calling from? Many of my clients would like to believe that!

One of my clients, a Sales Manager, had a rep who complained on a regular basis that the reason he was not producing results was the horrible prospect list he was given to work from. My client agreed with him that the list wasn't a good one and promised to get him a better list. One week later my client gave him another list. When he checked in with his rep and asked how the new list was working for him, his rep was delighted with it. The new list was much better and he was now able to schedule meetings. My client had given him the same list. It was actually his attitude, his own beliefs, that were getting in the way.

THE OLD TOXIC LANGUAGE OF SALES

The language they taught you to use in sales will affect your attitude. Many of my clients don't believe this until I repeatedly point it out. At one point they truly see the hidden attitude that is implicit when they use the old language of sales.

The most toxic attitude you could have is the attitude of "I want to GET something from you," i.e. "I want to get a meeting." The "I want to get..." attitude is one of the most damaging attitudes to bring to a conversation. You may think that you are hiding that agenda really well, or you may not even be aware that agenda is in the background of your conversation, but people are far more intuitive than you can imagine. Your prospects aren't fooled in any way. They can smell that agenda a thousand miles away and it doesn't smell good.

The traditional language of sales is about *getting* something, *influencing* or *persuading* your prospects. You need to *get* a meeting, a proposal, a sale, and *convince* someone that your product/service is a perfect match for their needs. We have sales *strategies* to force these outcomes. The question is: How would you like to be at the receiving end of a conversation with you when you are running those agendas? I am certain you have been in a conversation with someone trying to convince you to buy something. I have a technical term for those conversations..... ***ICKY.***

6

LANGUAGE IS FAR MORE THAN THE WORDS WE USE

Why have I chosen the title The New Language of Sales?
Julio Olalla sums it up perfectly:

"We have to start by realizing that we live in language in the same way that fish live in water: it is transparent to us. It's not that we don't know that we speak and listen, but rather we are unaware that language is *shaping* the world as we see it. When we see the sky after an astronomer shares with us distinctions about celestial bodies, we are able to see what we were unable to see before that conversation. We see galaxies, planets and satellites where before there were only a bunch of stars."

This happens to us all the time when we engage in conversations with people who share with us distinctions or information or insights we did not have before. You may think this is simply an example of learning new information. Learning information exists in language.

We are creatures of habit, not just physically but linguistically as well. Over the years we have been trained that the goal is to *pitch* your prospects, *hook* them, and *get* a sale. We have become so familiar with these attitudes and interpretations of selling that we may not even be aware that we are stuck in a manipulative and agenda-driven conversation. However, the general public is all too aware of that attitude and because of that they listen to us through the filter of "Ya, ya. All you want to do is get your hands on my money." Your prospects are all too familiar with the old school sales techniques. They have become resigned and cynical.

We also live with the illusion that we have conversations. In reality, most of the time our conversations have us.

7

LISTENING SKILLS THAT NO ONE TEACHES YOU

While we think communication happens in talking, it actually happens in listening.

Despite all the things they taught in school and in traditional sales training, no one ever taught us exactly how human beings listen and rarely, if ever, gave us tools that will take our listening skills to new levels of effectiveness. They did tell us that the prospect should be talking 80% of the time, but there are some far deeper reasons than simply uncovering their needs.

Listening is a critical factor in communication and essential for establishing trust and rapport.

First, let's define the difference between "hearing" and "listening".

Hearing is a function of biology.

One of the most remarkable things about this process is that it is completely mechanical. Your senses of smell, taste and vision all involve chemical reactions, but your hearing system is based solely on physical movement.

Any source of sound sends vibrations or sound waves into the air. These funnel through the ear opening, down the ear canal, and strike the eardrum, causing it to vibrate. The vibrations are passed to the small bones of the middle ear, which transmit them to the hearing nerve in the inner ear. Here, the vibrations become nerve impulses and go directly to the brain, which interprets the impulses as sound (music, voice, a car horn, etc.).

Listening is a different process. Typically, we are oblivious to how we listen. Listening is a function of linguistics. Language is not a passive tool for describing the way things are. It is much more! More than description, it is a way to create, generate, take action and put into motion events and situations that would not have been put in motion had we not spoken.

Two simple examples:

1) You are following up by phone with someone you met at a networking event and you ask to meet with them Monday at 10am. If the prospect agrees you have now created a Monday at 10am that did not exist five minutes ago. Yes, Monday was going to happen like it was always going to happen, but out of nothing you invented a new Monday out of what you spoke today. You weren't describing; you were creating. You generated an event that was not going to happen until you spoke it into being.

2) Think of all the times a prospect said Yes to a proposal. What would your career be like if they had all said No? By saying Yes, you moved into certain possibilities, actions and results. By saying No, you moved into different situations and possibilities, action and results. The simple act of declaring Yes or No is not an act of describing anything. It is an act of opening certain possibilities and closing others, of entering into some situations and moving away from others. You generate and create out of what you speak. The great majority of us already know this, although sometimes it's so close we miss it. It's so obvious, we don't see it.

How many conversations are happening when we are in a meeting?

When two people are having a conversation there are actually three conversations happening.

One is the audible one that you can record and play back - the one that you can hear.

The second conversation is the one you are having with yourself. "He said he liked what I have to say. This sale is a slam dunk," or "I really don't care about this stuff."

The third conversation is the one your prospect is having with him or herself: "Gee, when will he/she stop talking?" "I want to get that report done" or "This makes sense."

The second and third conversations are private conversations.

Private conversations are based on our own feelings, concerns, opinions, assessments, judgments, assumptions, values, beliefs and standards.

The Ontological distinction "Listening" is complex. Not nearly as simple as just letting the prospects talk. *It's all about how we listen to them!*

There are three levels of listening

Human beings (yes all seven billion of us) typically listen at Level 1. They don't maximize the potential of the other two.

8

THE THREE LEVELS OF LISTENING

Level 1: Internal Listening

When people listen at Level 1, they are actually listening to their own private conversation. That's where their attention is. They may hear the words of the other person, but they are primarily aware of their own feelings, concerns, opinions, assessments, judgments, assumptions, values, beliefs, stories, needs, and itches. They may be nodding, and going "Uh huh", but inside they are saying things like: "I had an experience just like that", "This is starting to bore me", "I really want to get home to watch some TV", "I'm hungry; when was the last time I ate?", "I'm terrified I'll say the wrong thing and look stupid", or "I know exactly what they need". At level 1 we interpret, conclude, and assume.

Being at level 1 listening can get in the way of your own sales success. There are plenty of times in our lives when level 1 listening is perfectly normal – it's actually important for us to pay close attention to our own needs and opinions. For example, when the contractor is asking you how you want your kitchen remodelled. That's a situation that is 100% about what you want: your opinions, judgments, desires. And of course, it's essential that in any sales conversations your clients and/or prospects be at Level 1. Your attention must be fully on them: their lives, careers, what they want, where they are and where they're headed.

Level 2: Listening for emotion

We all know that people don't buy on logic; they buy on emotion. At Level 2 you are aware of the energy between you and others: the emotions that are present. You are also aware of how that energy is changing; you detect sadness, lightness, a shift in attitude. You are conscious of the underlying mood, or tone, or the impact of the conversation.

Picture two young lovers sitting on a park bench. They're both at Level 2 with their attention completely focused on the other person. They are two people completely at Level 2, listening intently to every word and "listening" for every nuance in the conversation. It occurs that they can read each other's minds and often will finish each other's sentences. We tend to underestimate the importance of emotion; that is why I have dedicated an entire chapter to this topic. (See Chapter 22)

Level 3: Listening for commitment

This can be the most challenging of all levels to achieve and requires practice.

Commitments are strong promises to yourself or others, ones that you intend to keep. They are tied into your values and principles.

At level 3 you are listening for what they intend to make happen. What they are actually heading towards. What's important to them? What do they desire?

For example: as a parent you are committed to giving your children the best life you can. No matter what parents may say in a casual conversation, their intention is to do what they think best for their children. They may *want* to buy that new fridge, but if they feel a post secondary education is important and are committed to saving for it, the fridge will not be the priority. No matter how well you may think you have uncovered the need for the new fridge, communicated the features and benefits of the new fridge and closed for the business, without commitment, you will be bombarded with "We have to think about it" and somehow they never seem to get back to you.

The most effective selling takes place when you, the sales professional, are at Level 2 and Level 3. There will be times when you will drop into your own Level 1 place. You will fall back into judgment and opinion about whatever is happening in the sale, and in effect, disconnect from the client. You might be analyzing your own performance, as in: "That was a stupid question to ask", or "That was a good question; I think they really like me." At Level 1, you might be pushing your own agenda – something with the best intentions of "helping the client" but may not be what the client actually desires. As a sales professional, the key is to notice when you are in Level 1 and find your way back "over there" with the client. Sometimes all it takes is asking a provocative, curious question.

So how exactly do you listen for emotion and commitment? What are the clues?

We have all been taught about body language, but you can actually listen for these clues. Body language is an outward manifestation of how we're feeling. The majority of coaching is done over the phone, so how do we know what our client's commitments are? We listen for them. We notice when their energy is up: a clue to excitement and a topic they care about. We listen for when their energy is down; something is concerning them. We listen for when they go all soft and squishy; they are dreaming about something important to them. These are the types of clues you will start noticing with your prospects.

You must also listen to their language.

Beware of the word "should". There is no commitment behind that word.

Whenever I hear someone say "I really should do that and I will get to it one of these days," my response is that my calendar says Sunday to Saturday; there is no "one of these days" on it.

My own personal *"should"* is that I should go to the gym, however, the first time I walk into the gym is to join and the next time I walk in is a year later to cancel my membership. I am obviously not committed to working out at the gym. I am, however, committed to the *idea* of working out at the gym. My actions are quite clear about that.

One of the most common "shoulds" I hear is that I *should* be tracking my prospect information and stats better.

You have a choice here: take responsibility that you have no commitment to tracking and let go of any should conversation. Just know there is a cost. Take a good look at the cost to your business. If the cost is greater than the discomfort of practicing a different way of being and doing, you can shift any story you may have with regards to why you can't/won't/don't track.

In order for me to identify what a client is truly committed to, I listen to the tongue in their mouth, but I watch the tongue in their shoes.

I listen for something they say more than once. Perhaps a word they repeat.

It's all in our listening.

You will actually be able to hear more than you can see in their body language once you practice these skills.

Value Propositions

They taught us that our value proposition will be exactly what is needed to engage someone and tweak their interest. By understanding the filters that human being listen through: "Is this important to me?" "Do I care about this?" and knowing about your prospect's private conversations like: "This sounds like a sales pitch", we can now see why communicating our value proposition is rarely as effective as we would hope it to be. We get stuck in the belief that if we just massage it, work on it, and wordsmith it properly, people will want to meet with us. Unfortunately it doesn't usually work that way. From time to time someone will show interest in your value proposition. Make no mistake, this is simply because you have somehow hit a bull's eye with regard to ·
what's important to them at the moment. When this does happen, ask a lot of questions.

The importance of your value proposition is for you to connect to your commitment and boost confidence. By knowing the value you bring to the table, right down to your socks, there is something intriguing and engaging about you. This is a big portion of your attitude. This is different than arrogance or bravado. Connecting to your passion, conviction and commitment is part of what I like to call "quiet confidence". Arrogance is an offensive display of superiority or self-importance: overbearing pride. It is quite the opposite of confidence, which is an internal awareness of your value and abilities.

If part of your value proposition is "Honesty" imagine how honest you would occur if you kept telling everyone how honest you are: Really, I'm as honest as the day is long. I promise. Yep, that's me, Mr. Honest! I would start thinking "Who is he trying to convince, me or him?" When, however, you are *being* honest and demonstrating honesty in every interaction you have with your prospect, the message will be received. I can't stress the importance of this Ontological distinction enough. Who you are *being*, your attitude, your beliefs - is far more important that what you are saying.

One of the newer approaches in sales, is the Consultative Model. The training is about what you are saying but doesn't go deep enough to help you understand that your success does not live "out there somewhere". It's not about what you say, it's about what you believe. As an Ontological Coach I support my clients' being able to identify their own feelings, concerns, opinions, assessments, judgments, assumptions, values, beliefs and standards. That gives them access to powerful conversations with their prospects that are far more effective.

An attitude of trying to *get* something from you prospect is toxic to any conversation.

I invite you to consider a far more engaging attitude: an attitude of offering. Our role as sales professionals is to OFFER our prospects a choice they didn't have five minutes ago. We create new possibilities for our prospects.

Creating Possibilities

By sharing new ways of looking at things, by giving your prospect new distinctions/information or insights and helping them see outside the box of their own beliefs, possibility is created. Your prospects can now see something available for themselves, their company, their career, their department, etc., that they didn't see available prior to your conversation. Something that is important to *them*, not necessarily to you. Even if you see something that's missing, a gap, for your prospect, if it's not important to them you can't make them care about what you think should be important to them. You can't convince them that they should look at things differently. It's about finding out what *is* important to them. They have to see it for themselves. This can be challenging. This will be where asking versus telling will serve you best. The quality of the relationship you build with your prospect is dependent on how well they believe you will take care of what's important to them. When possibilities are created that inspire our prospects they are far more likely to commit and take the steps required to make this new possibility become a reality. It has nothing to do with convincing and everything to do with inspiring.

This all sounds very nice, but how exactly do we accomplish it?

9

<u>FOUR ATTITUDES OF SUCCESS</u>

There are four main attitudes I believe will support you in achieving your goals: Contribution, Curiosity, Intentionality and Leadership:

1. CONTRIBUTION: The genuine desire to add value and/or make a difference. By managing any private conversations where you want to get something, and authentically look for places to add value, you will find your prospects start to tell you things that they probably would not have disclosed. Conversations that are free of judgments, assumptions or assessments will actually create and generate safety for your prospects. After all, it's not safe to talk to a sales professional.... "All they want to do is get their hands on my money by convincing me to buy something." They are guarded, just waiting for that slick sales pitch and objection handling technique.

2. CURIOSITY: Curious questions come from how you listen to your prospects. They don't come from a list of open-ended questions you wrote down. They come from an attitude of wonder. I wonder what motivates my prospect? I wonder what drives them to make the choices they make? I wonder what is truly important to them? I wonder why they just said what they said?

Three year olds are perfect examples of genuine curiosity. They may ask why the sky is blue. Once you answer that there is another question that was triggered by your response. Then another question. The three year old is genuinely fascinated with his/her line of inquiry.

The perfect example of this is from a client of mine. She is a master at the art of curiosity. We were traveling across the country and on the flight she simply asked the gentleman next to her what was bringing him to our destination. He told her he was going to see a specialist with regards to a health issue. Because she is genuinely interested in any person she talks to, within five minutes he had disclosed that he had a heart problem and was drawing her diagrams of the issue. At one point he looked up at her and said, "This must be boring for you, I apologize," and was about to put the diagram away when she said with complete sincerity "No, this is fascinating." He smiled and continued to talk and draw. How often have you seen someone disclosing such personal information to a complete stranger? This happens with curiosity. After all, I am my favourite topic.

3. INTENTIONALITY: Being intentional is staying focused on a goal. There are really two intentions we hold as sales professionals. The first intention must be to add value. There is only one area you can add value and that is in the area of the services you offer.

The other intention is to build your business.

I believe that to be effective at sales, the goals must be in that order: holding the prospect's priorities and goals first and foremost, not the other way around. Doing so will enable you to earn a lucrative income. When our intention is to get the business by offering our services, we are holding our own goals and priorities above theirs. Self-serving agendas are not very engaging or effective.

4. LEADERSHIP: The best definition of leadership I have ever heard came from Bob Dunham, of the Institute for Generative Leadership:

- Leaders declare a future that other people commit to
- Leaders connect to what people care about so that they commit
- Commitment has action which produces results
- Leaders build power: the capacity for action and to have things happen
- Leaders coordinate action
- Leaders make offers
- Leaders care
- Leaders are present, open and aware of who they're being
- Leaders have a presence producing trust such that people listen to them

How and when does leadership show up in a sales conversation? When you make requests. An example of that is simply asking the prospect what the next step is and where you go from here.
So what's the difference between leadership and being pushy?
If you are being pushy, it is for a self-serving reason. You want something from them. Leadership is about doing something because it is in the best interest of your prospect or client regardless of whether it serves you or not.
A project you are working on for one of your clients has developed a hiccup, and if not resolved in a timely fashion, will derail the project. If you contact the client and he/she says call in two weeks, you would

probably explain why this requires immediate attention and stay on top of it. That is leadership.

This attribute must be present in any sales interaction. It is demonstrating to the prospect what it will be like to work with you. When your prospect says to call them in two weeks, it is a leader's role to identify what day and time would be most convenient for them and schedule it. Send an Outlook invitation. That is demonstrating leadership.

It requires practice to embed any of these attitudes. The first step is to simply notice what is going on for you behind the scenes.

10

<u>SKILLS</u>

There are four basic skills I invite every sales professional to internalize. Having them ready at any time and putting them into use as automatically as possible will take all conversations to the next level of effectiveness.

These skills require PRACTICE, and practice requires time and rigor. You would not expect to become a black belt simply by reading a book. You have to get on the mat and practice on a regular and consistent basis for long periods of time.   Here's the thing about human beings.... we are fundamentally lazy.

All too often I see sales professionals try something new and if they don't develop mastery at it in record time, they throw their hands up in the air and profess, "See, that didn't work!"

Another attitude that I have noticed is one with a time limit on it. "I've tried this for three months, and it hasn't produced better results. See, it doesn't work!"

How long does it take to master any new skill? As long as it takes. I consider it all to be a learning journey. There is no destination, just the next level of mastery, and then the next level of mastery. Wherever you are at the moment is the perfect place to be; there's nothing wrong here, just new things to learn in order to enhance productivity.

What are the four basic skills needed?

Once your attitude is more in alignment with offering, the skills required to master effective communication may sound simple, but they are far from easy to master.

The skills are:

1. **Listening**
2. **Questions**
3. **Making meaningful offers**
4. **Effective requests.**

We've gone into great depth with regards to **SKILL #1: LISTENING SKILLS** in chapters six and seven. As mentioned, the questions you ask come from how and what you are listening for.

SKILL #2: QUESTIONS

There are four types of questions you can ask:

1. Engaging
2. Curious
3. Intentional
4. Stop you dead in your tracks

Engaging questions are questions that start conversations. I don't believe we need to go in depth with this line of questions. For those of you who have difficulty with this, one that I have seen open up conversations is "What's been keeping you busy these days?" This will give you insights as to what's important to that person.

I have given you my definition of **curiosity** in the Four Attitudes of Success (Chapter 9).

Intentional questions are designed to determine if you can add value in any capacity. For example, many of my clients are Financial Advisors. Most of them are very comfortable generating conversations with engaging questions but allow the conversation to wander, thinking that they are establishing rapport by discussing golf. By being present to the fact that they are not golf pros and much as they believe they may be able to help with their prospect's golf swing, that is not their core competency. A line of intentional questions may be asking where the prospect sees him/herself in five to ten years. They may plan to retire in Florida and golf five days a week. Now that is something a Financial Advisor CAN help with.

If you're in Real Estate, by finding out about their vacation plans, you might uncover that they would like to own a vacation property. You can't help them plan the vacation (unless, of course, you are in the travel industry), but you can certainly support them in finding their dream property.

If you are in the insurance industry, by finding out about their plans for their children you might uncover an opportunity to help provide for or even protect their children's future.

You must earn the right to ask **stop you dead in your tracks** questions. Your prospects must feel comfortable and trust you. They must feel safe enough to potentially look bad by answering that type of question. This type of question takes the concept of "thought provoking" questions to a whole new level.

The goal is to have your prospect's eyes open wide and think or say "Wow, I never thought about that!" These questions are more difficult to learn and implement.

They will vary from industry to industry.

A good example I can share with you is one from a client. Ann is a Financial Advisor and she plays bridge with a wealthy woman, Joan. Ann was concerned about jeopardizing the relationship. (In the next chapter I will go into detail about how to transition a social relationship into a business conversation without jeopardizing the relationship.) For this example I'll tell you how Ann earned the right to ask the stop you dead in your tracks question. While having coffee with Joan, Ann just listened. She practiced all the listening skills we were working on that have been identified in this book. By being curious, genuinely interested in Joan, and managing her own private conversations, Joan felt comfortable enough to disclose that she was selling her house because she no longer wanted the burden of real estate ownership. She was going to rent. Ann then asked if Joan had a financial plan (an intentional question). Joan disclosed she did not. Ann then asked the stop you dead in your tracks question... "Then how do you know how much rent you can afford?" Joan was stopped cold.

At one of my workshops my associate and I were demonstrating these questions and because I, like most of my sales peers, don't find a lot of value in role playing, I conduct real-play.

We just had a conversation at the front of the room. She asked me a lot of questions about my business. At one point I told her about my first year in business. I made every mistake an entrepreneur can make. I didn't scale back my lifestyle and earned $3,600. Yes, you're reading that correctly. Because she had no agenda and was genuinely curious and because I knew, beyond a shadow of a doubt that she cared about my well being, she earned the right to ask the stop you dead in your tracks question "What plans have you put in place to ensure you never go back there?"

I had an Exorcist moment. For those of you who remember the moment when Linda Blair's head spun around, that is exactly what happened to me. I was gobsmacked - completely dumbfounded, shocked, totally speechless!

This would have been a perfect opportunity to discuss a variety of services to support me.

A great example of how not to ask questions is someone I used to know quite well.

She knew that asking questions was a good way to initiate conversations, but her questions felt more like an inquisition rather than a conversation. What was missing was genuine curiosity and listening. She would ask the question, wait till my lips stopped moving and jump right into the next question she had in her head from the list of questions she thought would get me talking. She may as well have put a spotlight in my eyes and started to ask where I was last Thursday night, what time did I leave the house, when did I arrive at my destination and was I associating with any unsavoury individuals.

I would like to leave you with some homework with regards to questions and agendas.

Start to notice *how* people ask you questions and how inclined you are to answer them. Which questions have you start talking and notice the question, and more importantly, the attitude behind the question.

I can use my own sales as a prime example of the attitude that was behind a simple question and the difference it made to a cold call. I was calling corporate America to introduce my coaching services. One question I can ask is "Has anyone ever explained the many different coaching models that are currently in use?" Most of the executives I talk to are keenly interested and inclined to schedule some time with me. However, the executive I contacted at Benson and Hedges said, "You're rude" and hung up. After I wiped the sweat off my forehead and my heart rate went back down to the normal range, I did some self-coaching. I had asked that question about 50 times that day and on this one call I had occurred as rude. I have no commitment to ever occurring as rude. I noticed that I was running a private conversation of "You people in the corporate world *think* you know what coaching is but really, you have no clue!" The question was the same, but the attitude was different. As a matter of fact, I was being righteous, which occurred as rude.

SKILL #3: MAKING MEANINGFUL OFFERS

An offer is based on something that is meaningful to the prospect such that you can add value in that area of their business, career, department, or life.

Your ability to generate a new possibility for your prospect is closely linked to your ability to make meaningful offers and requests. Offers are a fundamental way we take care of each other, build relationships and ultimately build our careers.

Some of the things you offer are your time, experience, expertise and/or resources.

SKILL #4: MAKING EFFECTIVE REQUESTS

In sales we typically call this "closing". I prefer to use the coaching term "making effective requests". The pitfall in using the language of "closing" is the possibility of falling into an attitude of trying to get something from your prospect. Get the meeting, get the proposal, get the sale. The language we use truly drives our attitude. Shift the language and over time, your attitude, as well as your prospect's attitude, will change.

Effective requests have no "*process*" or clever *pitch* or slick *strategy* designed to *get* people to do things you want them to do. The traditional "closing" techniques miss the bigger context of how requests and promises are an integral part of building the trust that is so essential for relationships.

As mentioned before, the sales professional may be pushing his or her own agenda – something with the best intentions of "helping the client" but may not be what the client actually desires.

There is a layer of intentionality as well. Adding value and offering your prospects a choice they didn't have prior to your conversation is how you earn a living. There is no one who would begrudge you that.

There are five possible responses to your requests:

1. Accept
2. Decline
3. Counter offer
4. Commit to commit at a later date
5. Slippery response

If a prospect gets slippery this could be a clue that you simply haven't found what's important enough to them to move forward. Keep exploring by asking questions.

On one of my TeleSeminars I was demonstrating this process: listening, questions, and making requests. I asked one of the participants to simply engage me with a question and we'll have a conversation. More real-play. He asked what my goals were for retirement. Since I'm a business owner another good question could have been "Tell me what your goals are for your business." I proceeded to tell him about the difference between goals and dreams and that I had no real goals for retirement yet. He then asked about my dreams. He was genuinely curious and asked questions based on what I just finished saying. Before I knew it, Coach Willa had disappeared and Willa showed up. I started to talk about my dreams and went all soft and squishy. He let me talk for a minute or so and then in the softest and most compelling voice with a genuine attitude of contribution said "Let's make that happen." My response was "OK." At that moment I realized that I was being paid for this call and snapped back into the coach mode.

He demonstrated to the whole group how an effective request is the sweet spot of sales. No features and benefits, no value proposition, no hook. He found what was important to me by asking curious and intentional questions. By listening to me he heard my commitment, what I intended to make happen. He then made the request to meet based on offering me something that was meaningful to me.

Simple, but not easy.

In your own sales career, you have actually done this many times and probably just thought, "That meeting/call went well" and if I would have asked what exactly was it that went well, many of you would just say "We developed rapport" or "I uncovered his pain." You probably asked the right questions, were effective at listening for what was important and made a meaningful offer and effective request.

In the example of Ann and her bridge partner Joan, after Ann earned the right to ask the stop you dead in your tracks question "How do you know how much rent you can afford" and noticed Joan's response, Ann then made the offer to sit down with Joan and crunch some numbers with her. Ann then made the request to meet. Meeting scheduled!

11

<u>RESULTS</u>

Now that I have covered some basics, we can start looking at what is needed to get to the next level of sales success. Take a moment and think about what your goals are for the next year. Now identify where you are today. What's missing?

When I ask that question I usually get answers like, better time management, better territory management, more support, better sales materials, etc. What's really missing is... results.

As we described, what has to change in order to produce breakthrough results is any belief that is limiting your success.

PUTTING MEAT ON THE BONES

So far we have built the foundation of sales, the skeleton, the framework.

Here's the beef!

Transitioning a social conversation into a formal meeting

There are a couple of conversational tools that you can use to ensure you never jeopardize your relationships.

To describe the tools we will assume you are meeting at a social, community or charity event.

<u>First conversational tool:</u>

Ask engaging, curious and intentional questions. Keep the conversation "over there", their favourite topic. We already identified that unless they are trained, human beings listen at Level 1. They are listening to their own private conversations of "Is this important to me?" "Do I care?" They will tune you out in a few short seconds if they answer no to one of those questions. Refrain from telling them too many details about what you do. Since you are fully human and your favourite topic is you and your private conversation may be screaming "I'd rather be at the dentist at this moment than listening to his/her story...When's it my turn to talk?" Simply notice it and plug back in.

When you are listening to your own private conversation you are hearing what they say, but you are not listening and you may miss that all important clue to uncovering what's important enough to that person such that they will want to meet with you.

Listen for emotion and commitments. What's important to them? What do they intend to make happen?

There are a couple of places you can go when you are at this point in the conversation.

If you find out what is vitally important to that person and you can identify an emotion and if when they ask you what you do (most likely they will be polite enough to do that) and they are genuinely interested in knowing about your services (a rare occurrence indeed), be careful....don't let your private conversation of "Yay, it's my turn to talk" get in the way. Resist the temptation to tell them all about your company and services. The key is to know why they are interested so you can create a meaningful conversation. We are perfect question answer machines. You will have to learn how to manage that design element in yourself and capitalize on that design element with your prospect. Instead of telling, **ask...** what in particular interests them? Ask why they are asking. Ask what they would like to know. Once you know it will be far easier to schedule the meeting to discuss that further.

This scenario is rare. Don't fool yourself into thinking they are interested in what you do. If they are interested it's only in what you can do for them and until you know far more about their situation you are blindfolded, throwing darts in the wind hoping to hit a bull's eye.

If you request to meet too soon, the risk of them declining your request is quite high. The bottom line is that the general public is afraid that you will try to sell them something. The public has been trained. They know that your job is to get something from them. We're changing that, but it takes time.

If you weren't able to identify what's important enough to that person such that they would like to have an in depth conversation about that, we are at the point of requesting to meet for coffee or an informal meeting to know more about them. The request, as all effective requests, must be built on an offer of your time, expertise or resources in a way that's meaningful to your prospect. In this case, it will be offering your time and listening. Be genuinely interested in what they are telling you and let them know you would like to learn more about that, perhaps over a cup of coffee?

When you start to master this skill, meetings will come faster.

Second conversational tool:

At coffee, NO BAIT AND SWITCH please! Once again, engage them in a conversation and always keep in mind that communication happens in listening, not talking.

Ask curious and intentional questions. Listen for what's important.

If you are able to find it, request a formal meeting. In the previous example of Ann and Joan, Ann simply asked Joan out for coffee. At coffee, Ann listened for what was important to Joan, not what Ann *thought* Joan needed, made a meaningful offer and effective request. If you are unable to find "it", it may just take more time. When they ask about you, this is a golden opportunity to demonstrate integrity. Tell them that you asked to meet to get to know more about them/their career/their company, not tell them all about you, but if they would like to know more about what you do you would be more than happy to set up a formal meeting.

Be vigilant about the "YAY. It's my turn to talk" trap. You run the risk of occurring like all the other sales people they have met before. Their private conversation will probably be something like "You tell me you want to know more about me, but really you just want to sell me something. You're all the same."

If they accept your invitation to meet, you now have a permission-based formal meeting and they will feel comfortable seeing you at the next social, charity or community event.

Where many sales professionals drop the ball is at this exact spot. Have you noticed a trend of simply exchanging cards and saying you'll give them a shout in a couple of days to schedule that meeting?

There are two things to consider at this point in the conversation.

First, when someone is completely engaged in a conversation and can see something available for themselves, their career, their department, their future etc., they are now seeing new possibilities. Possibilities that they may not have even considered prior to you asking them some thought-provoking questions. This is the moment they will want to discuss it with you.

Schedule the meeting right then and there. We are living in the Blackberry world. Take it out and tell them that since we are all really busy it's probably best to pencil something in and ask what their schedule is like in the next few weeks.

If you wait and call them, that possibility that was uncovered could and probably will die off in short order. All it takes to forget about that new possibility is an email from the boss asking about the report that is due or even simpler… all it takes to have that new possibility die is for them to notice bird poop on their freshly washed car.

The other reason it's important to schedule the meeting right then and there is that it demonstrates leadership. You're being proactive.

The most common response to a request from a sales professional is to decline.

12

<u>THE DREADED NO</u>

I f you are one of the very few people on this planet who has no problem or concern about the word NO, congratulations. There aren't very many of you and you probably have been practicing and shifting your private conversation for many years.

For the rest of you, that word has significant meaning. It has the power to sabotage your success and prevent you from being all you can be in sales.

Know that you are not alone in this. Seven billion people are in the same boat with you (except those lucky few I made reference to). It's a human thing. We are hardwired to hear the word NO and interpret it something like "I've done something wrong here" or "I've said something wrong here" or "I should have done this" or "I should have said that." In other words we interpret it as... "There's something wrong here and that something is ME."

It requires a lot of practice to shift that private conversation. After all, much as we would like to believe that we are rational beings, our emotions actually drive us.

Here's the reality of being at the receiving end of the word NO. You are hardwired to believe it has something to do with you but, it actually has nothing to do with you and everything to do with them. Remember those private conversations? Their private conversations are all about their own feelings, concerns, opinions, assessments, judgments, assumptions, values, beliefs and standards.

Unless we ask we will never know what actually went on between their ears.

I'll share my favourite story. I heard it during one of my coach trainings so I feel compelled to let you know that I do not personally know either of these people and heard the story second hand.

A young man stole up all his confidence and asked a co-worker out to dinner. She declined his request. He hung his head, turned around and was about to walk away, but had been coached on this very topic and promptly turned back around and asked "Was it the dinner invitation you said no to, or was it me you said no to?" "It was you." As you can well imagine his confidence was plummeting downward. He then asked "Is it my personality? Because I thought we got along so well here." She answered that she truly liked him and would normally be delighted to go out with him, but he is a full head shorter than she is and being self conscious about her height, is uncomfortable with that. He then suggested that they meet at the restaurant and she come a bit earlier so they wound not have to walk in together. She thought that was a wonderful idea. They had such a lovely time at dinner she forgot all about the height difference, walked out with him and dated for a long period of time.

It takes courage to have that kind of a conversation.

When you make offers or requests, always keep in mind your prospect has those five possible responses:

1. Accept
2. Decline
3. Counter offer

4. Commit to commit at a later date

5. Slippery response

They can choose any of those responses. The reality is that most people chose to decline your offer and/or request. I believe that is a sound choice and will always respect and honour that.

As long as you can honestly say that you were not trying to manipulate, convince, influence while holding the intention of offering them a choice that was based on adding value, you have done your job and a great job it is!

13

HOW WE PROCESS INFORMATION

The "I know" conversation

How we observe situations determines what we see as problems, what we see as possible solutions, which drives our actions and produces results in alignment with this. This element of our human design can get in the way of effective proposals. We typically jump to conclusions about what we believe is important to the prospect and stop asking questions before we really find out the root of what drives their need. When you think "I know what they need" don't assume that *is* what they need.

The best question to ask at the end of your first meeting is "Of all the things we discussed today, what did you find most valuable?" If you only take one thing away from this book, make it that question. When you ask that question – here's the coaching – manage the surprised look on your face! I have found that eight times out of ten I am shocked by their answer. By the way, they have just handed you your second meeting, or even your sale, on a silver platter.

Have you noticed that a lot of your prospects have to "think about it" after you present your proposal? What that probably means is that you haven't found "it", that thing that's important enough for them to want to commit and take action on. You have probably identified what *you* think is important to them, and the difference could be night and day.

If we look at the facts, when a prospect has to "think about it", they are actually declining your request to move forward. At that time, they are a "No". This doesn't mean they will always be a "No".

From an Ontological point of view, let's take a peek at how you may interpret this statement. What do you make it mean? Do you interpret it as "They really see how great my services are and the sale is just around the corner"? My clients are usually upset when I point out that really, at that moment, the prospect was a "No" or they would have picked up the pen and signed the proposal.

What I wonder is: has my client lost track of what was truly important to their prospect? If so, the consequences could be what I call "The Chase Me Game". This is when your prospect gets slippery. They start to avoid, or they don't return your calls. They are in the "Catch me if you can" mode and are hiding behind any excuse they can think of "I'm terribly busy, call back next week" or "Call me in the New Year" or "I have to talk to my spouse or boss first."

What was missing was identifying what was important to them or a priority or what they were committed to, which would have had them want to move forward.

I have my clients explore what was present in conversations that had the prospect pick up the pen and sign. You created and actually generated a conversation that was meaningful to the prospect such that they were committed to moving forward. Most of the time how you did that is hidden from your view.

14

COLD CALLING

I would be remiss if I didn't write a chapter on cold calling. There are a lot of self-sabotaging and disempowering beliefs about this activity. The one I hear the most is that cold calling doesn't work. I bet you can find ten web sites and multiple books that have been written to substantiate that story. Oh yes, make no mistake, that is simply a story that someone believes like The Truth and has found a lot of evidence to substantiate it.

I have a term for those people who will sell you their CDs or book confirming that cold calling doesn't work and that if you just prospect *their* way you will have all the wealth you dream of.

I call them Merchants of Hope.

What I can tell you from personal experience and by having worked with hundreds of sales professionals it that cold calling can and does work if approached properly.

Being successful connecting with people on the phone has nothing to do with a magic script that hooks people and everything to do with who you are Being.

People don't remember your words, they remember your attitude. They remember your passion and when you plug into that, cold calling goes to higher levels of productivity.

The first distinction I want to make is the difference between a telemarketer and a sales professional. As a telemarketer, I am only interested in getting a sale from you, a totally self-serving mind set. You know when you are on the receiving end of this type of conversation. Think about the telemarketer who has called you in the past week or two. They are reading from a script, no passion in their voice. If they manage to keep you on the phone, by paragraph number three they assume you want to buy their product or service. If you throw an objection at them they quickly flip to page five in their manual and read the appropriate response.

As a sales professional, you are offering them a choice they didn't have two minutes ago, with the goal of adding value. If your attitude is "I'm not trying to sell you anything, simply inform you of my services should they be of value to you," people hear something different but most are not sure what it is.

The next layer of an effective cold call is being able to speak your passion. In coaching we call that speaking your truth.

What is it about your product or services that you truly believe would be a contribution to your prospect? Why are you selling what you are selling? If you aren't sure how to answer this, I would invite you to dig deep.

If I were to call ten of your top clients and ask them why they chose to work with you and your company, what would they say?

If they were to answer "Because he's a good guy" I would coach them to tease out what that means to them. By the way, this exercise is incredibly important to your ongoing relationship with your client. Whatever they tell you is what you want to give them more of.

The other important factor about that exercise is that what they tell you is actually your value proposition.

When you have identified what you are passionate about and that is present in your conversations, people are far more likely to listen to you. I have been cold calling since the early 80's and work with some of the largest companies in the country. When I ask them why they meet with me, the resounding answer is "Your passion".

It's contagious, and people are drawn to it.

As a successful business owner I get three to four cold calls a day. In the past 12 years I can only remember receiving four calls from sales professionals. The calls are different. I can hear that in three seconds. No script or hook, just someone interested in offering me something that might be of value to me.

The most memorable cold call I have received was from a sales professional working for a company that optimizes web sites. His introduction was "Willa, I'm a little nervous; I'm cold calling a Sales Coach." He had me. I talked with him for over ten minutes and when I told him that I had gone down that road and spent a considerable amount of money optimizing my web site with no results, he tried to help me, no hook no pitch, no script, just help. Asking if I had tried this or that and doing some research for me right there on the fly. A sales professional! I was so disappointed that I had no need for his services that I went through my database looking for leads I could give him. Let's identify why this call was so effective, and why I was so engaged.

Before I start, I want to give you a bit of a background on me. It is a challenge to sell anything to me. My private conversations are all about judging and assessing your sales skills. It is hard for anyone to get past that.

Having told you that, the reason he had me was that he was being honest, genuine and speaking his truth.... "I'm nervous." Many of you are aghast at the thought of being that open. As I have mentioned numerous times in the book, you can't hide that. We can all hear it in your voice. He was totally up front and his honesty was delightfully refreshing and engaging.

Next he was clear about his intent, to add value to my business. He then offered his assistance.

I use the word introduction, not script. The language I use for sales is intentional; it is designed to move away from getting and move into offering. Simply by changing that word in your vocabulary, your attitude will shift.

I believe words like hook, script and pitch only succeed in perpetuating the old perspective of sales.

The power of the language we use is fundamental to transforming sales.

What you say in your introduction is unique to your personality and passion. Even two sales professionals in the same company will probably have two very different introductions.

I wish I could give you the magic introduction, the one that will instantaneously make all your cold calls fabulously effective. The magic happens when you communicate your passion and you just talk authentically and naturally. Simple stuff, but by no means easy. You have been programmed by the old model of sales to believe that if you just say certain words, you will succeed. Not so.

One client told me her introduction and my request was that she never say that again. She was incensed! She proceeded to tell me how long and hard she worked on that introduction and had spent a lot of money to have it wordsmithed for her. I told her I had no doubts about that and that is exactly what I heard. An audio brochure. Something like, wa wa wa, sales pitch, wa wa wa, feature/benefit, wa wa wa, haven't I dazzled you enough to want to meet? I then asked her to just tell me about why she does what she does. At one point in the conversation I actually felt her passion, the hair on my arms went up. I told her that is what she should be saying in her introduction. She then told me she didn't know exactly what she said. My response was… good! Keep speaking from that place: from your passion.

The best way to engage a prospect on the phone is to introduce yourself and your company, speak your passion and ask an engaging or curious question.

Keep in mind: the longer you talk with a prospect on the phone, the less likely they are to meet with you.

Make the request to meet to continue the conversation once you have engaged them in a conversation.

15

<u>OBJECTIONS</u>

Part 1: On a cold call

You will probably be faced with many objections and there are as many objection handling techniques as there are objections. Why do some work and some don't?

It goes back to your attitude, your beliefs.

If you are simply reading from the script you will occur as a telemarketer.

The worst I have ever come across is a telemarketer who called my girlfriend during one of her dinner parties. I heard my girlfriend say very politely that she wasn't interested in that product. Objection handling technique #1 was delivered. Still polite, my girlfriend declined the offer. Objection handling technique #2 was delivered. A little perturbed my girlfriend explained that she had company and was not interested and wanted to get back to her guests. Objection handling technique #3 was delivered. My girlfriend lost it, got angry and hung up. The telemarketer's techniques were simply rebuttals. When you think about the rebuttal attitude, it really comes from the place of "I'm right about this, you're wrong and I need to sway you over to my way of thinking."

There is a powerful background conversation that human beings share. This background conversation is the belief...

I'm right.

We tend to listen so as to make our beliefs right. We love being right, and it shows up everywhere. What prevents many of us, you the reader as well as your prospects, from exploring new possibilities or being open to new avenues or taking new actions...*is our commitment to being right.* The attitude of "I'm right, therefore you must be wrong" is a fundamental Ontological distinction describing who you are Being. Being right is such a strong desire for human beings that we will put our lives on the line and kill others, all for the sake of Being right. We would rather be right than be happy and successful.

Being right and making someone wrong is not an engaging attitude.

An engaging attitude *is* the Ontological difference.
When you are genuinely curious about their objection and have an attitude of wonder, the likelihood of them opening up is far greater. After exploring the root of their objection, speaking your truth, speaking your core beliefs, sounds logical.

I work with major corporations. I know when they say that they have already allocated their budget for the year and to call back in the fall, that's when I speak my beliefs (not like its right, just like it's what I believe): if that is the case my timing is perfect! That we should meet now. Why does that work? Because what I know to be true is that if we meet in the fall and they believe that my programs would be in alignment with their initiatives moving forward, the fall is too late to make that happen. It would probably require many months of exploring synergies and defining budgets in order to move forward, so the spring is when they really should decide if this is something they want or not.

This is not objection handling technique #35a. I manage any background attachment I may have. The communication is agenda free and they usually agree to meet with me.

Most sales professionals would just call back in the fall.

So here you are, plugged into your passion and eager to offer your services to everyone on that list sitting in front of you. So why does the phone weigh 75 pounds? Why are you thinking you'd rather stick a pin in your eye than pick up the phone and make that phone call?

16

PROSPECTING RELUCTANCE: THE FEAR OF SELF-PROMOTION

"The thick-skinned fearlessness expected in salespeople is more fiction than fact. It turns out that many salespeople are struggling with a bone-shaking fear of prospecting. This fear tends to persist regardless of what they sell, how well they have been trained to sell it, or how much they personally believe in the product's worth."

"The fear of self-promotion is the general condition which makes call reluctance possible in salespeople. It's found everywhere in motivated, goal-striving people who have trouble promoting themselves. Not limited to salespeople, it keeps competent and deserving people in many walks of life from being recognized for their contributions and, therefore, from earning what they're worth."

"The notion that call reluctance is a single condition is a venerable piece of nonsense which has largely been discredited. Twelve different types have been identified so far and there are probably more."

> Excerpted from, *The Psychology of Sales Call Reluctance: Earning What You're Worth in Sales* by George W. Dudley and Shannon L. Goodson, ©2007, Behavioral Sciences Research Press, Inc., Dallas, Texas. USED WITH PERMISSION.

There are many assessments available to sales professionals and anyone who knows me knows that I believe the only thing they are good for is pigeonholing people. Just because someone is outgoing does not mean they are well suited to sales. I believe personality assessment to be an inaccurate indicator of your sales success. There is one assessment, however, that I do recommend. Know that I receive nothing for this recommendation other than the knowledge that your blind spots will be illuminated with regard to any self-limiting belief, giving you powerful tools that will support you in blasting through any barrier to your success.

You can find the assessment at www.salescallreluctance.com.

Are you willing to look? Many people would rather stick their heads in the sand or avert their eyes. It takes courage to look at the barriers holding you back. If you are having private conversations like "I don't need any of that", "That stuff never works", "I already know this stuff", "I've already done assessments", "I have no time for this", then I invite you to consider those are exactly the beliefs that will hold you back from achieving your full potential.

As human beings we are typically afraid to take a good look in the mirror to identify what is really going on for us behind the scenes. By and large the reason is that we are afraid that it will identify something that is wrong with us. This could not be farther from the truth. Getting to the next level of productivity requires seeing what is holding you back, not like you are wrong, bad, or broken. There is nothing wrong with what I call your "stuff". By identifying what holds you back you own "it". When it is hidden from your view, "it" owns you. The bad news it that by identifying it, it doesn't go away. The great news is that by identifying it you now have the ability to shift your belief, which will give you new avenues for productive actions, producing breakthrough results.

Are you ready and willing to look? Then one place to start is with the following self-assessment.

Take a few minutes to answer each of the following questions as honestly as you can. Each requires a simple "yes" or "no" response. Write your answers on a separate piece of paper.

CALL-RELUCTANCE® SELF RATING SCALE

1. I probably spend more time planning to prospect than I devote to actual prospecting. Yes or no?

2. I'm probably not really trying to prospect for new business as much as I could or should because I'm not sure it's worth the hassle any more. Yes or no?

3. I probably don't try as often as I could to initiate contact with influential people in my community who might be prospects for the products or services I sell, or at least a source for referrals. Yes or no?

4. I get really uncomfortable when I have to phone someone I don't know, who is not expecting my call, to persuade them to buy something they may not want to buy. Yes or no?

5. Personally, I think having to call people I don't know, who are not expecting my call, to promote a product or service is humiliating and demeaning. Yes or no?

6. To me, self-promotion doesn't really bother me. I just don't apply myself to it very purposefully or consistently. Yes or no?

7. I try to avoid giving presentations before groups if I can. Yes or no?

8. Actually, prospecting doesn't really bother me. I could initiate more contacts if I were not involved in so many other activities which compete for my time and energies. Yes or no?

9. I find myself hesitating when it is time to ask for a referral from an existing client. Yes or no?

10. I tend to need time to "psych" myself up before I prospect. Yes or no?

11. I tend to spend a lot of time shuffling, planning, prioritizing and organizing the names on my prospecting list (or cards) before I actually put them to use. Yes or no?

12. Regularly making cold calls (calling on people I don't know who are not expecting my call and who many not want to talk to me) is really difficult for me. Yes or no?

13. I tend to feel uneasy when I prospect because deep down I think that consistently promoting yourself or your products is not very respectable or proper. Yes or no?

14. To me, making sales presentations to my friends or asking them for referrals is unacceptable because it might look like I was trying to exploit their friendship. Yes or no?

15. I often feel like I might be intruding on people when I prospect. Yes or no?

16. To me, making sales presentations to members of my own family, or even asking them for referrals, is inappropriate because it might look like I was trying to selfishly exploit them. Yes or no?

17. It is very important to me to find innovative, alternative ways to prospect which are more professional and dignified than the methods used by other salespeople. Yes or no?

18. I think that prospecting for new business probably takes more out of me emotionally than it does other salespeople. Yes or no?

19. I do OK in one-on-one sales situations, but I would probably get really nervous if I found out that next week I had to give a sales presentation in front of a group. Yes or no?

20. Highly educated, professional people like lawyers and physicians tend to annoy me, so I don't try to initiate contact with them even though I probably could if I wanted to. Yes or no?

21. Self-help material, like this self-rating scale, is superficial and probably won't teach me anything I don't already know. Yes or no?

22. I have reasonably clear goals, but I probably spend more time talking about them than working towards them. Yes or no?

23. I would probably feel more positive about prospecting for new business if I had some additional training to fortify my product knowledge. Yes or no?

24. I probably could prospect more, but I'm really just marking time until I get to do what I *really* want to do. Yes or no?

Scoring Your Call Reluctance Self-Rating Scale

Compute your overall call reluctance score by adding up your "yes" responses. Then read the following interpretive summary which is based on your total number of "yes" answers.

Total Number of "Yes" answers	Interpretation
1-2	**PREVENTABLE**
	Indicates one of two conditions: Either you are experiencing no emotional difficulty whatsoever associated with prospecting, or you really are experiencing some distress but you're hesitant or emotionally unable to reveal how much, even to yourself.
3-4	**MANAGEABLE**
	Indicates that you are like most other salespeople. The fear of self-promotion is present but only in low, non-toxic amounts. It may be occasionally annoying but it is not likely to be serious if it remains at this level. It should be manageable by simply emphasizing the markets and prospecting techniques you are most comfortable with and avoiding those which are the most threatening. The book, *The Psychology of Sales Call Reluctance: Earning What You're Worth in Sales* , however, is still recommended, because it can

strengthen your tender prospecting areas, and by so doing open up even more prospecting possibilities later.

5-6   LOW TOXIC

You probably have moderate levels of call reluctance at the present time. One or more forms of call reluctance are currently limiting your prospecting activity to a level beneath your ability. Low prospecting probably keeps you from exploiting the potential of your market. If so, reading *The Psychology of Sales Call Reluctance: Earning What You're Worth in Sales* should be personally and financially rewarding.

7-8   HIGHLY TOXIC

Your answers indicate a considerable amount of call reluctance at the present time. Your prospecting may be only a shadow of what it could be or needs to be. But don't despair. Instead, fasten your seat belt and get ready for some serious self-confrontation.

9 or more   SEVERLY TOXIC

Do you glow in the dark? According to your score, you could have enough call reluctance to stop a small sales force. Are you comfortable making calls on *any* prospective buyers?

One other interpretation is possible. You may be too self-critical. When you took Abnormal Psychology class, were you certain you had all the pathologies described? In church, are you the sinner the clergyman accusingly preaches to? When you complete a test or rating scale like this one, do you think most of the self-critical statements apply to you? If you suspect you might have been too hard on yourself, ease up. Go through the scale again.

If you found this information valuable and/or interesting, I encourage you to research their web site and determine if the full assessment and books would be of value to you.
www.salescallreluctance.com

What are the 12 Faces of Sales Call Reluctance?

I would not do the complexity of this topic justice by writing a brief explanation of them all. The book *The Psychology of Sales Call Reluctance: Earning What You're Worth in Sales*, by George W. Dudley and Shannon L. Goodson, ©2007, Behavioral Sciences Research Press, Inc., Dallas, Texas, always sits on my desk.

The categories are:

Doomsayer
Over-Preparation
Hyper-Pro
Stage Fright
Role Rejection
Yielder
Social Self-Consciousness
Separationist
Emotionally Unemancipated (not what it sounds like)
Referral Aversion
Telephobia

(And my old Way of Being:) Oppositional Reflex - Hard-edged type of call reluctance characterized by need for continuous feedback which is then criticized and rejected as invalid. These salespeople are unable to allow themselves to be coached, advised, managed or trained.

Thank goodness I possess sales DNA ... I succeeded in spite of this.

I have always been a top performer in sales, but I can't even imagine the breakthrough results I would have achieved had I been coachable.

Better late than never.

17

EMPLOYING ONTOLOGY - YOUR KEYS TO SUCCESS

Many of you have purchased some of those CDs or books describing the new sales "process" or "strategy" that promise to triple your sales almost overnight. You may have tried on some of the "techniques" and you may have found them successful *for a time*. From an Ontological point of view your first key to success and producing breakthrough results starts when you shift out of the First Order of Learning and explore the Second Order of Learning. Without shifting your belief, you will only find limited success in any new approach.

As in every aspect of sales the Ontological methodology of listening at Level 2 or 3 is the next golden key to success. By practicing your listening skills you will begin to develop mastery in questions that identify meaningful offers and requests.

With practice you will start noticing emotion and commitment, the elements needed to forward the conversation.

Notice how often you are listening to your private conversation, thinking of a good question to ask or plotting and planning what you are going to say next in order to get their interest.

When my clients start practicing all these distinctions they tell me how much easier and comfortable the conversations are. And how much more effective they are.

18

EXPECTATIONS THAT KILL CONVERSATIONS

K eep a look out for conversation killers. One is an expectation of "in order to". "I'm going to do or say this, in order to get that" is clearly Level 1 listening, not where you want to be. This expectation will make the average person want to escape the conversation. You actually occur as pushy, desperate, needy, greedy, etc.

Are you attached to an outcome?

A client, Robert, was concerned about the fact that he had no trouble scheduling meetings but when it came to the proposals he was bombarded with "I have to think about it". We've explored the possibility that when he heard that, it might mean he wasn't able to find out what was important enough to the prospect such that they wanted to commit to moving forward.

In Robert's case what I heard was an attachment to getting the sale. There is a difference between attachment and commitment.

Attachment is when you are locked into a certain outcome and you will do anything in your power to get that outcome to materialize.

Something like how a pit-bull grabs onto something and locks his jaw onto it. Short of anesthetising him, he won't let go. Attachment is where you will try to force the outcome. Ever notice what happens when you are in a conversation where you feel someone is trying to force the outcome? You'll resist, avoid, or even defend. This is not how you want to leave your prospects, with the response of resisting or avoiding. If you ask me, that sounds a lot like the Chase Me Game. Hold on to attachment long enough and you may be going down the road of resentment and anger. Keep a vigilant eye out for it.

Commitment is like plugging a destination into your GPS system, letting go of control and trusting you will get there. You are committed to an outcome, that destination, but have no attachment to how and when it will materialize. You are intentional about why you are having the conversation, but there is no background desire to force the outcome. You are simply exploring the opportunity with no expectation. Your GPS system, your intentions, will get you there while you sit back and enjoy the journey.

While I was explaining this distinction, Robert had an Ah Ha moment. He identified that he had an expectation and attachment. When he assumed he knew exactly what the prospect needed, the proposal would be a slam dunk and they would move forward. He then shaped the entire proposal meeting around that, pushing and forcing the outcome he assumed would take place, and was surprised when they didn't jump up, grab the pen out of his hand and sign anything he put in front of them. He then thought about the sales that *did* move forward and his attitude was very different. He was clear that his services could add value, but not certain about what they needed. He kept defining what the prospect needed and actually was quite certain they wouldn't sign. He became very curious and surprise, surprise, those where the meetings that the prospect chose to work with him. We identified what went well in those conversations. His commitment to adding value to those prospect was the destination he plugged into his sales GPS. He had no desire to force an outcome. He let go of control and the ride was very enjoyable.

It is easy to fool ourselves that we know exactly what our prospect needs: that our solutions are the right ones and in the best interest of our prospects.

Sometimes we can be seduced by the brilliance of our own solutions – the brilliance may be in our own eyes only. It is easy to delude ourselves into believing that the prospect will automatically see the brilliance of our solution and accept it unquestioningly (as well as fall at our feet for the penetrating insight we just presented).

19

TRUST

Although dictionary.com defines trust as:

1. Reliance on the integrity, strength, ability, surety, etc., of a person or thing; confidence.

2. Confident expectation of something; hope.

3. Confidence in the certainty of future payment for property or goods received; credit: to sell merchandise on trust.

4. A person on whom or thing on which one relies: God is my trust.

5. The condition of one to whom something has been entrusted,

I could ask ten people what trust means to them and I would get ten different answers.

The best definition I have found comes from a coach training.

By the way, this isn't the truth, just one way of looking at trust.

The training has broken it down into four categories:

- Sincerity
- Competency
- Reliability
- Tuned in

Sincerity will be assessed by how genuine the prospect feels you have their best interests at heart.

There is no concern about saying something and not meaning it. When someone says they will do something and we later find out they were half-hearted about it or never intended to do anything, the intensity of our emotional response can be quite high. In some way we may feel not only hurt and angry, but also invalidated as human beings.

Competency is how well they believe you have the experience, expertise and/or resources to fulfill on your promises.

Reliability is assessed by how well you have kept your promises and/or commitments. This is also linked to your integrity, doing what you say you are going to do and if something derails your commitments (and these things happen all the time) there is no problem as long as you communicate this to your prospects as soon as you are aware of them. If you have committed to putting a package of information together and getting it to them by Friday and on Tuesday you identify that you will be unable to fulfill on that commitment, you communicate that on Tuesday, not Wednesday, Thursday or Friday.

Every commitment is accompanied by explicit and/or implicit expectations about standards of performance, i.e. assessment of the quality of the final outcome. Not meeting required standards for performance generates mistrust and damages what is possible in relationships.

Trust is not only an assessment we make about the present, but also about the future. People can be sincere in making a promise and at the time of committing were genuine in their intention to take the agreed action. However, they may then do their reputation enormous damage by not being reliable in managing their promises. Being impeccably reliable in taking care of clients' needs has become a key ingredient of competitive advantage.

Being tuned in is how well our prospects feel we understand what's important to them. This is when we assess that others are empathetic with what is important for us.

Your words may be fine, but you may be operating for the position of "I know just what you need" and inadvertently pushing your own agenda. Prospects can easily confuse this dimension of trust with insincerity. You may be sincere in agreeing to take some action, but you are not as fully tuned in to the prospect's needs as they would like. In short, they may assess that you do not have the level of emotional participation that they would like.

Your "gut" feelings will be a help with this. Sometimes your prospects will be telling you about what it is they need, but your gut may be telling you "That's not it". Stay tuned in and keep asking questions to identify what truly is important to your prospect. When you find it, you will notice that their attitude shifts. Trust your instincts. They rarely fail us.

If an advocate or prospect forms a negative assessment in one of those areas, they will most likely declare they "don't trust" you. When we don't trust someone we can usually find at least one of those things missing. Either I assess that person isn't sincere when they say they'll do something, or I assess that person isn't competent to do what they say they'll do or I assess that person has broken so many commitments in the past that I can't risk another one this time.

Trust always involves risk, because no matter how well I try to assess the situation, the other person may take new actions which are different and unexpected. The person I extend trust to may let me down.

How long does it take to build trust? I have the definitive answer to that. Anywhere from five minutes to....never give up! It takes however long it takes.

One of the traits that many sales professionals share is the desire for instant gratification. I notice it in myself, the private conversation of "Let's get a move on here.....I put it all on paper for you yesterday. Why didn't you sign it on the spot? Let's go!!"

From an Ontological point of view, this private conversations stems from "It shouldn't be like this. It should be different. There is something wrong here." This private conversation will lead to nothing but frustration and suffering.

The instant gratification gene can get in our way in two forms.

First, your prospect will, no doubt, pick up on your private conversation of "Let's get a move on". You might not speak those words, but they can hear that attitude nonetheless. It's as loud as a foghorn.

Second, it can serve as demotivating and hold you back from probably the most important and successful part of the sales process, the follow-up.

It no longer surprises me when I hear "If they haven't signed in X months, I just drop them from my database." BIG MISTAKE!

The message you are sending is "I'm not really interested in developing a relationship with you. If I can't get my hands on your money/budget, I'll just disappear. I'm actually not very reliable and not committed to your needs, just to my wallet." This is the general perception I am passionate about shifting.

The only thing for you to do is notice and manage it. Stay focused on the bigger picture: what's important to your prospects. It's going to take however long it's going to take and there's nothing wrong with that.

20

<u>ADVOCATES</u>

So we are all on the same page, what I define as an advocate, or centre of influence (COI), is someone who you have built trust with such that they are comfortable introducing you to their friends, family or associates.

One of my clients, Sheila, came to a coach call with a concern; many of her potential advocates think she wants to "sell" them something and they are reluctant to meet.

The question I asked was "What exactly are you selling them?"

WHAT EXACTLY ARE YOU SELLING TO AN ADVOCATE?

I believe we are selling long-term relationships based on trust and respect. Any advocate has to trust and respect you before they are willing to introduce you to a client, associate, friend or family member. Sheila is in financial services and is clear about her passion, which is helping people to achieve their dreams, and her commitment, which is to generate a successful business. And we identified that ultimately she is OK with the perception she is faced with because she completely understands that creating a relationship based on trust and respect TAKES TIME. It takes time to shift the perspective and concern that "You're just trying to sell me and my friends something."

If you genuinely want to get to know more about the advocate, their business and goals they will hear that. This is an area that employing the insights I have talked about, building trust, being curious, and of course being intentional will be valuable.

There is a lot on your plate here. When you practice and master these, the payoff is well worth it.

To walk in and have one or two great conversations and expect them to introduce you to their clients is a pretty optimistic.

One of the foundations of Ontology is taking responsibility for how your attitude and actions impact others. If you meet with an advocate a couple of times and neglect to stay in touch on a regular basis, what is the message you're sending?

"Hi. I *SAY* we want to get to know you and build a reciprocal referral relationship, but *REALLY* I just want to *GET* a referral from you and if you don't give me one quickly I'll just disappear."

Who you are being is someone who is insincere and lacks credibility, and without that the impact will be mistrust of you. You can certainly harbour resentment (see chapter 22) if you provide several introductions to them and they don't reciprocate, but by asking yourself where you dropped the ball on generating trust would be a far more productive way to further the relationship.

The professional I hired to help me edit this book, David, told me that his real estate agent calls him a "Partner for Life". I like that phrase.

One concern I have heard is not being able to refer business to an advocate, with the associated belief that the advocate won't want to do business with them, so the sales professional doesn't approach them. At this point in the book, this should sound familiar to you.

Belief = I have nothing to offer

Action = not approaching the advocate

Result = A big fat O.

Here is another approach.

The best connector I have ever come across, Donna Messer,
demonstrates the power of connecting people when she speaks.
She does her homework and finds out who she knows in the audience.
She then calls on them.

This is an example of what she does.

Donna – "Joe, are you here?"

Joe – "Yes."

Donna – "Joe, what are you looking for?"

Joe – "An admin assistant."

Donna – "Is there an admin assistant here that is looking for work?"

Carol – "I am."

Donna – "Joe, meet... what's your name, Dear? (Carol) Joe, meet
Carol."

Donna – "Carol, give Joe one of your cards."

Carol – "I don't have any."

Donna – "Carol needs a printer. Is there a printer here?"

A master connector! Learn from her.

Once you build that relationship and they have given you an
introduction, how do you thank them?

Thank your advocates the same way you would thank any referral.
The nicest note I have ever seen is "Thank you for your trust and
confidence in me." Include a personal gift. One that says "I know what
you're interested in and it's important to me to remember." If they are

an avid gardener, perhaps a book on gardening. If they are family oriented, perhaps a family pass to a movie. It doesn't have to be expensive, just meaningful.

At one of my workshops a very successful Advisor shared his approach to accountants.

Although this approach is geared towards Financial Advisors, we will look at the approach in detail to see the elements of each conversation and why and how it works so well.

He meets with each and every one of his client's accountants and asks how they want the tax paperwork to come to them at tax time. Exactly what paperwork they want, in what order… down to the smallest detail. Although this does create more work up front, at tax time his associates are not fielding 10-20 calls per day.

After tax time he has a conversation with each accountant and asks how that went and if they need to change anything for next year.

He then looks at them straight in the eye and says "My goal is that *all* of your client's paperwork comes to you like that every year."

Let's look at this approach in detail:

- I have always wondered why accountants are not keen on creating reciprocal referral relationships. I think it's because they are not people people. They are numbers people. They are happy in the back room wearing a visor in front of an Excel spreadsheet. He has identified the biggest stressor in their business and life: tax time.

- He then OFFERS to help them by GIVING of his time and energy with a clear goal of making their lives a bit easier at tax time.

- He's being intentional... he's clear about why he does this. He wants to build his business and not one accountant has begrudged him that.
- He makes effective requests: based on meaningful offers.
- He's in ACTION. No inner dialogue of "That's a good idea, I *should** do that one of these days.***"
- He produces extraordinary results.

*Notice any shoulds in your life and stop shoulding yourself
**I don't know about you, but my calendar says Sunday to Saturday, no "one of these days" on it.

21

<u>FOLLOW UP</u>

Thimis is where most people fall down. I find that many sales professionals have a timeline in their head and if the prospect hasn't agreed to move forward they drop them.

I'm asked fairly regularly how long it takes to move from first contact to new client? I can say definitively, I have the answer to that… One hour to NEVER GIVE UP!

How long does it take to identify a gap or something that's missing that would add value?

How long does it take for the prospect's situation to change such that there is now a possibility to work together?

How long does it take to build trust?

I wish I had the crystal ball to predict all that.

I'll share with you the best follow up verbiage I have ever come across. When having the initial conversation, let them know the day and even the time you will call to follow up. The reason you are calling is because you are a person of integrity and do what you say you are going to do.

<u>Message #1</u>

Hi ___, this is _____ from _____ calling because I promised to reach you today. Sorry I missed you. My number is _____. If I don't hear from you by ___ ill try again on _____.

Message #2

Hi ___ , this is_____ from _____ calling, because I promised to reach you today. Sorry I missed you. I notice that you've been difficult to reach and I'm not sure if it's because you're really busy or I've been guessing the wrong times that you might be at your desk/at home. If you wouldn't mind letting me know how to proceed, that would be great. My number is _____ .

Message #3

I noticed that it's been _____ since the last time we spoke. I am now facing a dilemma and I need your help. If I continue to call, I run the risk of becoming a nuisance, but if I stop calling I am sending you the message that I'm not interested in working with you, which isn't true. Please let me know how you would like me to proceed. I can be reached at _____ .

22

<u>REFERRALS</u>

I'm sure you are inundated with emails and offers from many sources with tips, hints, and verbiage you can use to get referrals. According to their marketing information you can actually be a millionaire in about three weeks if you just buy those books and CD for $79.95.

More Merchants of Hope.

You know you should ask, but *knowing makes no difference.*

If you have ever been a pound or two overweight, I am sure you know what to do to lose the weight, reduce your calorie intake and increase your calorie output. Sounds so simple doesn't it? However knowing this makes no difference when you are watching your favourite sporting event on TV, eating a bowl of nachos with yummy melted cheese and chili (or those of us with a sweet tooth, we would have our hands in a box of cookies or caramel popcorn).

Until you address what makes you uncomfortable asking, there are no books, CDs or workshops that will make a difference. This applies to any part of the sales conversation that you are uncomfortable with.

With all the information available to you, giving you more techniques won't make a difference until you uncover WHY you don't ask. You must find the story or interpretation you believe that has stopped you from being effective in this area.

I suspect that much of our discomfort relates to the typical referral conversation that was designed in the old manipulative model of sales training.

"Do you feel my services have added value?" YES. "Who do you know that can benefit from my services?" I CAN'T THINK OF ANYONE. "Why don't you take out your address book and let's start at the A's." I have actually been at the receiving end of this conversation. It's still alive!

OR the famous piece of paper.

"Do you feel my services have added value?" YES. "Just take a minute a write down all the people you know who could benefit from my services." Then put a piece of paper in front of them with five lines on it and look away.

Yet more ICKY conversations.

You don't want to be at the receiving end of these and most people certainly don't want to be at the delivering end of these conversations. So over time most sales professionals went to the other extreme, just dropping a bunch of hints and hoping for the best.

"If you know of anyone who could benefit from my services please give them my card." And then we give them a stack of cards hoping that they will bring them everywhere and hand them out.

Sound familiar? How well does that work? Not really well at all.

I'd like you to consider what I think is the most important element of asking for referrals… the same theme throughout this book, shift the conversation from getting to offering.

It's about offering your time, expertise and resources to your client's friends, family and associates in order to make a difference to them or add value or help in any way you can. Completely different conversation. This conversation leaves your clients feeling important and honoured. It's all about your attitude and the context of the conversation.

There are really only three reasons you don't get the number of referrals you'd like:

1. You just don't ask – because you let concerns stop you

The most common concerns that stop many sales professionals from asking for referrals.

a)   Don't want to put clients on the spot

b)   Avoid discomfort for them and you

c)   Rejection – The dreaded No

> You've done a lousy job

> They could say something negative

2.   You're inconsistent

3.   You're ineffective at asking

Hopefully we've addressed #1 now by shifting perspectives from getting to offering and by noticing any concern, and by practicing asking, you will start to become more comfortable. You do have to give yourself permission to be a learner, make mistakes and learn from them. If your private conversations are telling you why asking for referrals won't/can't work for you, I invite you revisit the chapter on Friends of Learning (Chapter 2) and take on an attitude that is a friend of learning and let go of any attitude that will work against you.

We'll look at #2 and #3 in a minute but first let's look at why clients don't refer.

They: -Can't think of anyone

-Don't talk business with people

-Don't want to feel liable if things blow up which would reflect badly on them

-Fear lack of control – many people are very uncomfortable when they let go of control

-Don't get feedback – not knowing what happened once the introduction was made.

Only 20% of people have what is referred to as **Referral DNA.** These are people who love to connect people. People like Donna Messer.

Because I have referral DNA, I know that we get pleasure by connecting people.

If you fall into the 80% that are uncomfortable connecting people, don't let your concern/story (see chapter 2) get in the way.

Here's the homework: tag all your clients, friends, associates or advocates who have given you introductions/referrals in the past 12 months. They have referral DNA.   Here's the coaching: give us a lot of pleasure by allowing us to give you the gift of connecting you to others. It truly is a gift we enjoy giving!

2. Inconsistency

The people who don't have referral DNA are uncomfortable connecting people no matter how compelling the offer is. For those people consistently making the offer and request is the name of the game.

It's not your client's job to remember all the services, expertise or resources you bring to the table. It's your job to remind them.

For these people, it's about a gentle consistent reminder. Keep making the offers.

3. Being more effective at asking

What exactly is included in an effective referral request? As I have discussed in Chapter 10 the first step is to make a meaningful offer which leads to the effective request for introductions.

Now let's look at what you can say that's in alignment with all these elements.

23

THE ART OF THE CONVERSATION

As with all the Ontological distinctions I have written about, effective conversations start with the attitude of contribution/offering and being intentional.

You can start a conversation by stating that you have been talking to a lot of people these days about (insert topic here).

Ask if they have been having these types of conversations.

Ask about their circles, work, friends or family. Listen and ask curious and intentional questions. Listen for opportunities to add value to their circles.

Let them know that you would like the opportunity to share some information or resources with that person and ask how your client would go about making the introduction.

You may ask "How would you feel comfortable making the introduction?" It may be in a social context, perhaps over coffee or lunch.

That dreaded NO may show itself here. Manage that private conversation of "There is something wrong here, and that something is me." All you did was make an offer and they declined.

This, like all new conversations will take practice. One of my many coaches describes confidence as simply being practiced at what you are doing. It makes total sense.

Maybe your client just gives you a name and phone number and says to give them a shout. Now what do you say?

<u>Phone Introduction to referral</u>: Mr. Client and I had a conversation and your name came up.

Ms. Client didn't tell me anything specific about your situation but he felt that because our company has such comprehensive services that there might be some value for you in knowing more about it.

Ask curious questions– get them talking.

<u>Potential referral introduction letter</u>

While we have not met, my friend/client, (name) speaks very highly of you.

(Name) and I have been working together and (he/she) has been extremely pleased with what we have been able to accomplish. (He/she) thought that there might be some value for you in knowing more about our services/company.

I would appreciate the opportunity to meet with you and plan to call you the week of (date) to determine if our services would be of value to you/your organization.

If you have any questions or concerns in the mean time please do not hesitate to give me a call.

24

<u>MORE OBJECTIONS</u>

When there is a belief that your opinion is right, a judgment or assessment behind your words, I hate to sound like a broken record but the prospect will pick up on it. Don't fool yourself, there is no hiding it. You may occur as pushy, aggressive, desperate, needy, etc. Each person will interpret it in his or her own way, but make no mistake they will know there is something going on behind the scenes and get uncomfortable. Welcome to Objectionville! You've heard many times that objections are simply a concern, and the way to move past them is to ask questions. Yes, there is a concern. Yes, we want to uncover the root of the concern and when you seem to be circling the airport, asking questions and just going around in circles without identifying the issues, the concern may be you and your hidden agenda!

Curious questions will be your best friend here. You are hardwired to want to justify, rationalize and explain, to *tell* your prospect all about your point of view. This can work, but it is a limiting way of being. Manage your human design to convince, force an outcome or be right and ask more questions.

An attitude of acknowledgement will also be extremely valuable here. There is a vast difference between acknowledgement and agreement. Typically we have these two distinctions confused. Many people believe that if you acknowledge something, in this case an objection, you are agreeing with it, so your instinct will be rebuttal. I'm right; let me prove you're wrong.

You can acknowledge someone's point of view without agreeing with it. Acknowledging someone's point of view, their objection, will defuse any potential defence mechanism they could employ. Rebuttal can create a pissing match.

When you acknowledge their point of view and when they get that you get their point of view, when you speak your beliefs, they will far more open to hearing you.

This isn't about "mirroring" your prospect or just repeating his/her words. When your prospect gets that you get them, you will see their energy/attitude shift. They will relax.

The ability to just be with your prospect wherever they are, like there is nothing wrong, nothing needs to be changed and there is no place to "get to" will create an environment where they are comfortable disclosing what is really going on for them behind the scenes.

Many of my clients simply don't know what types of questions to ask. They are far more comfortable making statements.

"Your price is too high."

"What is it about our pricing that concerns you?" Notice who you are Being when you deliver that question. If you have a judgment in the background, that will show up in perhaps an accusatory or arrogant attitude. You have been taught that your tone of voice is important. No matter how calm and "nice" you think your tone of voice is, if you are running an "in order to" or "I'm right and must convince them of that" inner dialogue, your prospect will hear it. Just be curious.

Practice answering questions with a question. Some of you will be thinking "The prospect will see through that in a second and know I'm up to something." The reality is if you *are* up to something – i.e. trying to manipulate them – they *will* see through it. If you are genuinely curious about why they asked that question, they will answer your question.

A possible way to avoid the "I have to think about it" objection is to ask: "Of all the things we discussed today, what did you find most valuable?" Once again, here's the coaching:

Manage the surprised look on your face when they give you their answer! My private conversation about what I think was sheer brilliance with regards to my presentation, is rarely what they found valuable.

The answer to that question will give you the direction you need to take the conversation. It will illuminate what is important to your prospect.

25

EMOTIONS

U h oh, this is the place that we dip into that feely-touchy stuff. I promise I will not ask you to hug anyone or talk about your feelings.

Most of us are very uncomfortable in this arena and yet standard wisdom is that people don't buy on logic, they buy on emotion. Exploring the realm of emotion will give you deeper insights into what this means and how deep this runs.

If we take a minute to look at the history of civilization we can see that the prevalent thinking has been that reason defined the achievement of humans and emotions interfered with clear, rational and logical thinking. Emotions were often considered dangerous and likely to create confusion, and did not allow for sensible decision-making and behaviour. Recently we have been expanding that old perspective to include the importance of emotions.

Humans are emotional beings. Much as even the most analytical people I know, engineers, will need to analyse data, graphs, charts and spreadsheets, at the end of the day, they will buy on emotion. (Don't tell them this; it may offend their sensibilities!) What I have experienced many times is their ability to rationalize, justify and explain their illogical and totally emotional decisions.

On the other side of the table sit your emotions. If you try to ignore your emotions and don't address what is going on behind the scenes, it will almost certainly get in the way of your effectiveness. Remember: Denial (De-Nile) is not a river in Egypt.

When you choose to expand your perspective and look at new ways of approaching sales, it does not mean the way you have always done things is wrong or that you are in need of "fixing" in any way. Washing machines need fixing, human beings learn and grow.

Perceiving, observing, thinking, listening, decision-making, speaking and physical movement are all actions. The quality of our actions is heavily influenced by emotions.

Understanding your own emotions and those of your prospects has the ability to greatly enhance or be enormously detrimental to any sales conversation.

As human beings we experience numerous emotions on a daily bases. They come and they go. Don't resist learning from them and about them.

We can't control circumstances. For example, being caught in traffic. What you can control is how you choose to deal with it. The traffic jam will not magically disperse because you lean on your horn and allow your blood pressure to rise while wondering what idiot caused this whole thing. (Yes, I have indeed been to Manhattan many times.) You can instead listen to some great music and enjoy the down time. What I do know from my coach training is that many times it doesn't occur to us that we even have a choice to make. "But I'm late for a very important meeting!" You will be late whether you get frustrated and angry and flip the bird to the person honking their horn or if you smile and think about your next golf game. Of course, being people of integrity you will communicate to your prospect or client that you're running late.

So how do emotions affect your sales and even your blood pressure?

The three emotions that are conversation killers are resentment, resignation and anxiety.

There are continuums for each of these three emotions.
On one end of the continuum is resentment.

When resentment is present, your private conversations may be something like:

- I have been treated unjustly or unfairly

- It should be different

- I did not deserve this

- I'll get back at, or punish them

You may be tense and defensive.

Think about what it would be like if resentment was in the background of your conversation. You may occur as a jerk or aggressive or perhaps a bull in a china shop.

On the other end of the continuum is the attitude of peace.

Private conversations coming from a place of peacefulness may be like:

- That's just how it is
- I don't like it but I can't change it
- I'll be flexible and open to a range of ways of looking at this situation

Think about a how engaging and enrolling a conversation with your prospects would be when peace is present.

Then there is the Resignation continuum.

| Resignation | Ambition |

When resignation is present there may be thoughts or stories like:

- Why bother doing anything
- What's the point of taking action
- Whatever

You will probably be disengaged and shut down. You've probably given up.

Think about what it is like to have a conversation with someone who has given up. You could very well occur as lacking confidence in your product, service, company or even worse, in yourself. Your prospect may think you won't be in this job very long, that you won't make it.

The other end of the continuum is ambition, with attitudes like:

- This can be done
- Anything is possible
- Let's do it
- Optimism

- Forward thinking, goal actualization

These are the ways of Being that inspire confidence.

I recently watched a documentary on consultants. One consultant was extremely open and forthcoming. He shared that he truly didn't have the type of education or background required to step into a major corporation and offer the services that he does, but what I noticed he did have were all the attitudes of ambition, and he has a consistent stream of lucrative business.

| Anxiety | Wonder |

The third major emotion is Anxiety, with a Way of Being like:

- I fear the future
- I will not be able to cope
- I don't have the capacity to deal with this
- I must protect myself from the worst
- Withdrawal

How you may occur to your prospect as a doomsayer, a fear monger, a Negative Nelly, a complainer.

On the other side of this continuum is wonder:

- I'm not sure what is going to happen and that's OK
- It will be interesting to see how this unfolds
- The world is a fascinating place
- Enquiry, curiosity, exploration

For a sales professional, this is truly one of the best attitudes to have.

This will allow you to really explore what's important to your prospects.

What is in the background of your communication IS your communication.

Jerk or engaging, unconfident or a go-getter, doomsayer or curious.

Let's turn the tables now since there are two human beings in this conversation.

It is equally important for you to be tuned into your prospect's emotions.

When any of the three emotions are present for your prospects, they will be doing their jobs well and killing off the conversation.

Be aware of their emotions: that's Level 2 listening skills. If you are at Level 1, busy listening to your own private conversations, you will miss the opportunity to see where your prospect's emotions are. Do you sense resentment? You might ask what you can do given that you can't change the current circumstances.

Is there some resignation behind what they are saying? You could ask them about their goals and what's important to them.

Do you notice anxiety? You may want to brainstorm ways to think outside the box.

As a sales professional, it's your job to listen like no one else has ever listened before. If there is an emotion like anxiety, resignation or resentment in the way, it's your job as a Sales Professional to notice it, acknowledge it, resolve or dissolve it. This is not a nice-to-have talent. It's critical for engaging your prospects, creating possibility and inspiring them to take action.

If you made it through the section on emotions, congratulations. You now have new insights on how and why they play a tremendous role in your sales success. And I hope you have some important tools that will support you in uncovering any emotions that could sabotage your conversations.

26

ROLLING IT ALL UP

We have discussed active listening skills, intentional questions and making meaningful offers and effective requests. The ball is in your court now.

Where do you go from here?

At this juncture, as with all paths we travel in life, you have many choices available to you. If you continue to do what you have always done, you will always have what you've already got. If this is the path you choose, I encourage you to be content with what you have, no complaining and no pity parties, please.

You can choose to use circumstances as an excuse and be the victim of them, or you can rise above them.

If you want to "think about" all of this, I invite you to ask yourself what results in life you have produced by thinking about things (a bit fat O).

If you choose to try on some of these new distinctions, give yourself permission to practice, make mistakes and learn from them. Those of you who fall into this category please keep this in mind:

When new learnings are incorporated and there is discomfort, productivity dips. Without reinforcement, you will most likely fall back on old behaviours.

Be vigilant and you will master these new distinctions.

Manage the instant gratification gene we all possess. Mastering any new behaviour takes time and practice.

My goal has been to show you that the Ontological approach is dramatically different and has a profound ability to produce breakthrough results, by understanding the basic principles of Who you are Being and how the stories you make up limit your actions and results.

So my friends, this is not the end, but in fact a whole new beginning. The entire foundation of traditional sales training is crumbling around us and out of it the new you will emerge: a far more effective, engaging and by the way, happier, and more satisfied sales professional. Welcome to your fulfilling new sales career!

May your journey be all you can imagine and may you experience joy and success along the way.

About the Author

With over 15 years' experience in Sales and 12 years' experience in sales coaching, Willa Silver brings with her comprehensive, hands on understanding of Sales and Prospecting.

Willa has been working with several of the largest financial services firms in Canada for the past six years, coaching and supporting over 550 Advisors in growing their businesses. She assists Advisors in defining their unique selling style, creating and practicing new approaches that support the Advisor in achieving and surpassing their goals.

Willa's first passion is coaching and she is a graduate of The Coaches Training Institute, an International Coach Federation accredited coach training school, and is continuing her coach training with a focus on Ontological coaching. Willa sat on the Board of Directors of The International Coach Federation for seven years.

Willa's second passion is sales and still actively sells her coaching services. The relationship with her current clients started with a cold call.

15424335R00064

Made in the USA
Charleston, SC
02 November 2012